GOOD GROUND
GREAT
HARVEST

GOOD GROUND GREAT HARVEST

BRIAN P. LUCAS

© 2025 by Family Priority Publishing

All rights reserved. No part of this publication may be reproduced, distributed, or transmitted in any form or by any means, including photocopying, recording, or other electronic or mechanical methods, without the prior written permission of the publisher, except in the case of brief quotations embodied in critical reviews and certain other noncommercial uses permitted by copyright law.

All Scripture quotations are from the King James Version of the Bible.

Brian P. Lucas is not a licensed and/or registered rabbi, preacher, bishop, priest, deacon, minister, teacher, theologian, seminary student or attendant, psychologist, therapist, or counselor and is in no way, shape, or form promoting a man-made religion, denomination, or church and/or providing you with any earthly religious advice in any capacity. All subject matter provided herein is for spiritual informational purposes only. Brian P. Lucas does not guarantee you results. You and only you are responsible for what you do or don't do with the spiritual and biblical information provided, so due diligence on your part is an expected and appreciated requirement.

Family Priority Publishing
66 W Flagler St
Suite 900 PMB #10522
Miami, Florida 33130

ISBN:
978-1-7324104-1-1
10 9 8 7 6 5 4 3 2 1

Printed in the United States of America

Lifetime Thanks

To Jan G. Lucas, who believes in me, cares for me, and loves me unconditionally, even when I do not know or understand how to believe in, care for, or love myself — a strong woman who has the eyes to foresee the person I am today, discrediting and contradicting the rest of the world, who told me I would be either in prison or dead by the age of 21. She is a caring woman who has loved me for me from the very beginning, not for what she could get from me, because I can assure you that I had nothing beneficial or productive to give when we met.

Jan sacrificed her time and energy to a lost and hopeless child who was full of pain and bitterness toward the world and everything in it because she could see his potential to become a man with something to offer. She willingly endured the growing pains of a boy as he matured and learned to become the man full of wisdom, knowledge, and power that she always knew was within.

Jan is an independent and self-sufficient woman who refuses to settle for less or accept mediocrity, no matter the circumstances, with or without the approval of others; a natural-born leader who understands the importance of being quick to hear and slow to speak; a silent but deadly opponent at the snap of a finger; an empowering and encouraging woman who always reminds me to use the negatives from my past to create a better future and tells me that the greatest way to silence the doubters and naysayers is simply to succeed.

Jan is a soldier, always hands-on, never sitting on the sidelines. She is a true representation of the support any real man needs to stay focused and continue to push forward through each phase of life.

Jan says what she means and means what she says.

She loves and trusts God and is a true representation of who and what she believes in, even till her death.

Jan brings light to the dark, smiles to the sad, joy to the brokenhearted, love to the hurt, strength to the weak, and hope to the hopeless; to say she has a strong work ethic, excellent morals, great character, and a magnetic and cheerful attitude would be an understatement.

Jan is the most Christ-like of anyone I have ever encountered in my life, a true woman of God who is full of faith and walks what she talks!

Jan, I need you to know that I love you, I miss you, and I am eternally grateful for every investment you made into my life that has undisputedly played a major role in making me the man I am today.

I will always love you, Jan, and I will see you again.

BRIAN P. LUCAS

Dedication

I dedicate this book to every one of you who has invested your time and energy into reading it and is seriously interested in implementing the changes required to be the best you that you desire to be and to be all that God has ordained and sanctified you to be.

Congratulations on taking a step forward toward improvement for yourself and your family and allowing me to be a part of your journey.

I wish you the very best to truly succeed in all your endeavors, and I encourage you to keep reading books, learning new things, and exposing yourself to experiences that challenge you to make sacrifices and implement changes that ultimately promote elevation, growth, and development.

I strongly encourage you to use this time as an investment with the hopes of achieving a huge return. To do so, you will need to eliminate any distractions and make reading, studying, and comprehending each chapter of this book a priority.

Thank you for granting me permission to speak into your life. I assure you that I will be 100% real with you on all levels; I will be very blunt, holding nothing back and telling it just like it is through the duration of the book.

I look forward to your success as you take this journey one chapter at a time.

To Your Good Ground and Great Harvest,

Brian P. Lucas
BRIAN P. LUCAS

Table of Contents

Lifetime Thanks v
Dedication vii
Tilling Good Ground xi
Foreword xiv
Make It Personal xvi
Introduction xix
Chapter 1: The Way Side 1
Chapter 2: Stony Ground 17
Chapter 3: Thorns 35
Chapter 4: Good Ground 57
Chapter 5: Great Harvest 87
Appendix 111
Bonus Chapter: Beware of the Leaven 113
The Conclusion 125
About the Author 127

Tilling Good Ground

Over 20 years ago, I met a man who changed my life in a way I would never have imagined, through our Lord and Savior Jesus Christ.

I met Brian in 2002. My first impression of him was that he was rude and stuck up and had a bad attitude. Like Paul in the Bible (which fits so well seeing how his middle name is Paul), little did I know that this man I highly disliked would become my mentor, best friend, and the love of my life.

God places certain people in our lives for a reason, and He doesn't care whether you approve of the relationship or not. Everyone goes through trials and tribulations, just like Jesus did, and I was no exception.

Brian was placed in my life at the perfect time. It was a time in my life when obstacle after obstacle was coming my way, so much that it could have destroyed my world and my life, but God had a plan, and that plan had a name: Prophet Brian PAUL Lucas!

Brian has helped me get through so many hard times in my life by teaching me to utilize the most important instruction manual known to man: the Bible. He has been a great teacher, pouring countless hours into me, helping me understand God's Word and God's Kingdom.

Through the Word I have learned seven important principles:

1. **Salvation** (Romans 10:9-10)
2. **Kingdom Purpose** (John 18:36, Luke 17:20-21)
3. **Trust God** (Proverbs 3:5-6)
4. **Love God** (John 3:16, 1 John 4:19)
5. **Have Faith** (2 Corinthians 5:7)
6. **Pray** (Matthew 6:9-13)
7. **Unity** (Ephesians 4:3-6)

I am so proud of Brian and the measures he has taken to pour into others through his books. I pray that through his written purpose, at least one life has been changed, just like God has used him to change my life.

I am blessed and forever grateful that God chose to place one of His strongest and most loyal soldiers in my life.

Thank you, Brian, not only for pouring into me but for also loving me, and for being a light in my life and showing me that I can do ALL things through Christ who strengthens me! I love you!

Tilling Good Ground,

LISA M. MARRERO
Kingdom Ambassador

My Prayer:

Father God, in Jesus' name I thank you Lord for Brian. I thank you Lord for utilizing your Prophet to spread the word of your Kingdom to the world.

I thank you Lord for being a bright light in my life, and I thank you Lord for always loving me even when I don't love myself. Without you Lord, I would be nothing.

I thank you Lord for the love and blessings you have given to me.

I pray Lord that you continue to speak through Brian and continue to utilize him in spreading the word.

I thank you Lord for all that you do. I praise you, I love you, and I glorify your name.

In Jesus' name, Amen!

Foreword

God has blessed you with another year:

- What are you going to do with it?
- What will you do to grow and evolve to be a better you this year?
- What will you do to put God first in every area of your life this year?
- What will you do to live a life more pleasing to God this year?

This is your year filled with the power of choice. What will you do with it?

MAKE IT THE BEST YEAR EVER!!!

I will do everything I can to be the best wife I can be. I am not perfect, but I want to be exactly what God has designed me to be in your life, nothing more and nothing less.

I am not God, nor can I (or anyone else) fill the void that is meant for God and God alone.

I do hope you strive to seek after God to fill that void and emptiness because you have been trying to fill it since before I ever knew you, and it is the last piece of the puzzle.

Your life will never be whole until you trust God with everything you have got and allow God to take complete control over you, holding *nothing* back.

From the day you were born until now, God has never allowed you to encounter any situation you were not already equipped to overcome.

Foreword

Those encounters were purposeful, to prepare you to be the strong man of God that you are destined to be. They were all part of your training battlefield.

The abuse, abandonment, drugs, alcohol, gangs, women, etc., and everything surrounding each situation was all a part of the plan.

Nothing was by accident. It was all purposefully allowed to shape and mold you to be a *strong warrior* and to know and recognize the tricks of the enemy.

<u>**The Devil is extremely crafty; you must take heed of this.**</u>

Anything that does not line up with God's Word is a ***trick of the enemy***; thus, situations that appear harmless and good on the surface bring about sin.

You have been hand-picked, put through the fire, and groomed. You have the war wounds from each trial to remind you of what needs to be done to defeat the enemy as you face these evil spirits in other people. This is why the Devil fears you so greatly and has been working overtime to keep you asleep, busy, and distracted!

Trust God with everything you have and let go of the world.

Walk in the Spirit and the mighty power that God has given you to dominate.

You are a powerful force, and God has been awaiting your arrival to lead His people.

I love you, Brian P. Lucas!

JAN G. LUCAS
Music 4 Christ Records
07/12/1975 – 05/01/2017

Make It Personal

I strongly believe that it is difficult to understand information provided to you, that is for you, if you do not make every effort to internalize it and Make It Personal.

Although for the majority, this style of writing may be considered unorthodox, I have invested the time to make sure that you are able to easily apply this information to yourself first.

Throughout this book, I will be using a lot of the Bible as confirmation and revelation, and in the process, I will be encouraging you with scripture to Make It Personal.

I personally have come to realize that it is so much easier and more beneficial and productive when I include myself and Make It Personal when reading the Bible. Instead of it just being someone else's story, it becomes my own, and it seems to become clearer and more concise when applied in this manner.

At the end of each chapter, you will be provided with each Bible verse that was mentioned and the opportunity to Make It Personal.

For example:

1 John 4:4

You are of God, little children, and have overcome them: because greater is he that is in you, than he that is in the world.

Breakdown:

You are of God, little children, and have overcome [the enemy and opposition]: because greater is God that is in you, than [the enemy and opposition] that is in the world.

Make It Personal:

You are of God, (Your Name), and have overcome [the enemy and opposition]: because greater is God that is in (Your Name), than [the enemy and opposition] that is in the world.

Insert Your Name on the lines below:

You are of God, _____, and have overcome [the enemy and opposition]: because greater is God that is in _____, than [the enemy and opposition] that is in the world.

I chose this specific verse because the subject matter in this book is not information the enemy and opposition necessarily want you to know.

Be prepared for that small, irritating voice that attempts to hinder you from obtaining truth over the lie, seeing the light amid darkness, and ultimately maximizing your God-given gift to fulfill your purpose. Prepare yourself mentally for a lot of pushbacks, even within yourself. For the majority this will seem like new information, but it has been right there in your Bible the entire time.

Closed eyes do not see, and plugged ears do not hear.

I strongly encourage you to explore the opportunities available to you when you begin to apply wisdom, knowledge, and understanding in a way that resonates with you immediately by making it personal to you in real time while reading.

A lot of times, information is overlooked, misunderstood, misinterpreted, and confusing, simply because we do not Make It Personal to ourselves; sometimes it hits harder and resonates more quickly when we add self to the equation.

I appreciate the opportunity to speak into your life. It becomes so much more powerful when you Make It Personal because you are then speaking into your own life, and there is no one better than you to do just that.

To you Making It Personal,

BRIAN P. LUCAS

Introduction

The church is walking blindly because their vision has become clouded by things of the world that do not align with God's will.

The shepherds have set their sights on success, money, fame, and power, which have become their gods.

Rather than doing God's will and allowing God to provide, they have chosen to use God's name as a platform to forge their own wealth, on the backs of God's people.

They have given in to compromise and church traditions for personal selfish gain, which has allowed the enemy to walk in through the front door, sit in the front row, conjure up distractions, and wreak havoc in the house of God.

Thus, the sheep are lost. Many have perished, while others lack wisdom and knowledge and continue to live in spiritual bondage.

God is raising up a radical army with unconventional eyes to see and perfectly tuned ears to hear God's voice. They will possess special gifts to navigate through the maze of deceit that the leaders who walked before them fell victim to. They will be a light in a world full of darkness, to lead God's people in these last and final days.

The shift has taken place, and no longer will you be able to depend on the platform of a church building and the person behind the pulpit as your only source of truth.

Pay attention to the calamity and the destruction and the compromise of what was once considered the norm and realize how God is using abnormal, unconventional, and somewhat unprecedented means to reach people.

Many of these people are those who will probably never visit a church building again, due to too many demonic, satanic, and ungodly reasons to mention here.

Church Hurt is real, and there are so many victims of those who proclaim to be representatives of God but cause more harm, hurt, and pain to others, both in the church and out, than anyone else.

How is it that there is more love, respect, loyalty, code, unity, and sincere acknowledgement and appreciation in the streets than there is in the church building?

How is it that the main component and ingredient seems to be missing?

If God is Love, why is there so much hate, envy, jealousy, discrimination, talebearing, backbiting, gossiping, and judgment in the church? Simply because there is a lack of basic knowledge of the importance of the Good Ground and the Great Harvest.

The Truth is always the truth, and it usually causes hurt or anger before it helps; nevertheless, it's still the truth, and it is the truth that will make you free.

Your time is now to walk in your authority, dominion, and power and to be all that God has ordained and sanctified you to be as a representative and an ambassador of the Kingdom.

Sincerely and respectfully,

BRIAN P. LUCAS

GOOD GROUND GREAT HARVEST

Good Ground: Mark 4:1-20
Chapter 1: "The Way Side"

Parable:

Listen; Behold, there went out a Sower to sow: And it came to pass, as the Sower sowed, some fell by *The Way Side*, and the fowls of the air came and devoured it up.

Revelation:

The Sower soweth the Word. And these are they by *The Way Side*, where the Word is sown; but when they have heard, Satan cometh immediately, and *Take Away* the Word that was sown in their hearts.

Question:

How many of you have heard something that was supposed to excite you, pump you up, motivate you, and really make you think about seriously changing something in your life for the better, but in the same second, you were immediately steered in the opposite direction, either by your own thoughts of doubt or by someone else's that ultimately discouraged you and stole that very seed/word from you?

Thoughts Like:

- That sounds too good to be true.
- That will never happen for me.
- I wish it were that easy.
- This only works for (fill in the blank) people.
- I don't think I can do it.

- I don't have this or that to do it.
- I'm not good enough.
- I don't have what it takes.

Whether from your own thoughts or from an outside source, you are enabling the fowls of the air to devour your seed and allowing Satan to take your word, blessing, success, growth, abundance, and prosperity away from you.

A hard lesson to learn, but you are always your common denominator of both success and failure, and it is the decisions that you make or don't make that manifest your results. Sometimes it's best to get out of your own way and stop allowing fear and other people's opinions to define who you are.

You need seeds to fall on Good Ground, and *The Way Side* is most easily explained as the *Take Away* from the Good Ground.

If you hear and receive something good that may possibly resonate with you, then you must learn to not allow fear or a third party to *Take Away* these experiences from you.

Beware of the "Seed Snatchers" in your life!

Proverbs 22:10

Cast out the scorner, and contention shall go out; yes, strife and reproach shall cease.

Breakdown:

Cast out the disrespectful mocker, and heated disagreements, disharmony, and conflict shall go out; yes, strife and discord, disapproval, and disappointment shall stop.

Many people wonder why they don't ever receive any opportunities, but I challenge you to check yourself, to see if maybe the opportunities come, but you allow them to fall to *The Way Side*.

Things Like:

- A business venture or idea
- A job promotion or new position
- A beneficial relocation or transfer
- Investment and financial opportunities
- A new skill set or furthering your education
- Making amends with family or friends
- Repairing broken relationships
- Allowing yourself to love and to be loved

It is so easy to become a victim of this type of behavior because, for most circles, it is considered normal, which would make everything you're reading right now abnormal.

Too many people are broke, live in lack, have a poverty mindset, and continue to struggle with not enough, simply because they are too weak and naïve to cast out the "Seed Snatchers" in their lives!

A "could've, should've, would've" life is no life at all, so you must learn to choose the path and the direction that benefits you.

Only an unwise, insecure, misleading, dream-bashing, hateful, envious, jealous, disrespectful, and confused person flocks with "Seed Snatchers."

It is time we all *Man* and *Woman* up and start making purposeful strides to step in God's greatness and really walk the walk, and stop just talking and letting fear and the "Seed Snatchers" keep us in lack!

The Bible makes it very clear and instructs us to simply cast them out, but compromise and contradiction just seems so much easier to most people. This is why you must be able to recognize those around you who purposely stop your seeds from falling on the *Good Ground*.

You will never be more than what you choose to allow yourself to be:

- Cast out the Seed Snatchers.
- Cast out the fake and phony people who pretend to be for you while simultaneously sabotaging your success.
- Cast out the Doubters and the Naysayers and rid yourself of pessimistic ignorance.
- Cast out fear, laziness, complaining, excuse making, and the like.
- Cast out lack, poverty, and the "not enough" mentality and mindset that has been pumped into you from the time you were born.

It amazes me how everyone wants to "run" something, but it seems someone forgot to explain to them that you must *Learn* and *Know How* to "walk" first!

This is exactly why there is a world full of crippled sprinters out there, "running" nowhere fast and struggling to "walk" anywhere slow!

Just because tradition, religion, and culture promote a destructive enslaving mentality doesn't mean you have to participate and buy into it.

Keep in mind the Bible is not just some fairy tale story book with a bunch of make-believe characters and scenes to appeal to your entertainment. The Bible is real, and so is the Enemy of the Truth because he knows that the Wisdom of the Bible is the one and only way that you will ever truly be free!

John 8:31-32

Then said Jesus to those Jews which believed in [Jesus], If you continue in [Jesus'] word, then you are [Jesus'] disciples indeed; and you shall know the truth, and the truth shall make you free.

So many people are under the false impression that they are free because they have been victimized by the smoke and mirrors of this world and have been taught that places like America (The Land of the Free) provide real freedom, but only the *Truth* makes you free.

What is the *Truth*?

John 14:6

Jesus said unto [Thomas], [Jesus] is the way, the truth, and the life: no [person] comes to [God the Father], but by [Jesus].

- There is no **Way** without Jesus.
- There is no **Truth** without Jesus.
- There is no <u>beneficial</u> **Life** without Jesus.
- There is no <u>real</u> **Freedom** without Jesus.

When people have eyes to see, they understand that just because people may not have ropes tied around their necks, hands bound by restraints, and shackles on their ankles, it does not mean that they are free. Those with ears to hear know that it does not take ropes, restraints, and shackles to enslave a society.

There is no doubt in my mind that right now, as people are reading and trying to process this information, the Enemy of Truth is attempting to attack them with the <u>*Take Away*</u> method and push their seeds to *The Way Side*.

1 Peter 5:8

Be sober, be vigilant; because your adversary the Devil, as a roaring lion, walks about, seeking whom he may devour.

The less you know, the less of a threat you are to the Devil and his *agenda* because you will not attempt to stop what you don't know is coming.

Matthew 7:15

Beware of false prophets [false ideas, false thoughts, false feelings, false direction, false instruction] which come to you in sheep's clothing [looks good, sounds good, feels good, tastes good, smells good] but inwardly they are ravening wolves.

The wolves attack your emotions by way of your thoughts and feelings and ideas that encourage destruction to your success, distractions to sway you, and roadblocks to your growth and improvement, which is why you must guard your heart/mind.

Proverbs 4:23

Keep thy heart with all diligence; for out of it are the issues of life.

Don't expect some big red creature with horns or some scary demonic monster to come snatch your seed away, because Satan is so much smarter and more subtle than that. Satan works through the people you come in contact with, and it is usually those who are the closest to you, including family, friends, neighbors, co-workers, church members, classmates, spouses or significant others, and unfortunately many times those in positions of power whom you may respect and hold in high regard.

Positions Like:

- Government
- Preachers and priests
- Teachers and coaches
- Employers and managers
- Actors and actresses
- Athletes and entertainers

Think about it — it is those you most respect who have immediate access to your ears and are more than likely able to sway you in one direction or the other.

I feel confident that 80% of the people reading this book can think of one situation or circumstance that was presented to them, and immediately one of the aforementioned people stepped in to _Take Away_ the opportunity.

The only way to stop it is to prepare for it, and that begins with fully comprehending *The Way Side* and how it may affect you.

I completely understand if one may feel that this is so much easier to write in a book or speak about than to do, but is it really, or could that be just another crutch or excuse to justify personal lacks and failures?

The door of opportunities for a successful life is open to those who make a choice to enter and choose to live life.

Pride, arrogance, and ignorance are comparable to a person staring at this door, with the keys in hand, but still not willing to make the choice to enter. If you truly want more and need more, then you simply must do more; your will to do must meet, match, or equal the want and the need.

Making excuses will keep a person in *The Way Side*, and unfortunately that means the seed or Word is not reaching the Good Ground.

Do not underestimate the power that Satan is able to have in your life if you decide to allow him to have it. Not knowing and not being prepared is giving your power of choice away.

Remember, Satan knows the Word of God, and unfortunately, it seems as if he knows way more Bible than most people do, including Christians! Please read that sentence again because it is 100% Truth!

Satan utilizes the very scriptures in the Bible by way of contradiction to condemn and place blame and guilt on people, and it works because most people _DO NOT READ THEIR BIBLE_ for themselves, so they don't really understand.

Let's be blunt — it is extremely difficult to rightly divide the Word of Truth if one does not know the Word or the Truth or understand that both the Word and the Truth are one and the same!

John 1:1-4

In the beginning was the Word, and the Word was with God, and the Word was God. The same was in the beginning with God. All things were made by [the Word]; and without [the Word] was not anything made that was made. In [the Word] was life; and the life was the light of [all people].

This is why reading your Bible for yourself is such a pertinent and crucial practice that must be taken seriously. True Word delivered should really be more of a confirmation of something you already know, have read prior, or may have heard, but if you don't know for yourself, then there is nothing that can be confirmed.

Make It Personal: Joshua 1:8

This book of the law shall not depart out of (Your Name)'s mouth; but (Your Name) shalt meditate therein day and night, that (Your Name) may observe to do according to all that is written therein: for then (Your Name) shalt make (Your Name)'s way prosperous, and then (Your Name) shalt have good success.

Amazingly and shockingly [sarcasm], the Bible provides us with a full explanation of exactly how we can make our way prosperous and have good success:

1. **Speak** (Mouth)
2. **Meditate** (Thoughts)
3. **Observe to Do** (Eyes to See and Ears to Hear with Action)
4. **Then Prosper and Succeed** (Results and Outcome of Acting on God's Word)

Prosperity and Good Success belong to you and are the outcome and result when you speak the Word, meditate on the Word, and act on the Word.

Make It Personal: Psalm 1:2-3

But (Your Name)'s delight is in the law of the LORD; and in [the law of the LORD] does (Your Name) meditate day and night. And (Your Name) shall be like a tree planted by the rivers of water, that brings forth (Your Name)'s fruit in (Your Name)'s season; (Your Name)'s leaf also shall not wither; and whatsoever (Your Name) doeth shall prosper.

What good is a book full of knowledge to you sitting on the shelf collecting dust, if you never pick up the book and actually read it?

What power do you receive from the knowledge in the book if you don't even know what's in it?

An engine is full of power, but what good does it do for you if it is sitting idle?

What benefit do you receive from the engine if you never activate the power?

Thoughts, visualization, and speaking are power, but if you think, visualize, and speak about losing weight, running a marathon, or hiking a mountain and you never get out of bed or off the couch, then what is the benefit?

What power do you receive by thinking, visualizing, and speaking without taking action?

If you know how to catch fish, where to go fishing, how to set your fishing pole, and how to place your bait, will knowing this information put any fish in your boat or cooler, on your plate, or in your stomach?

How many fish will you catch just knowing the information if you never actually use it?

James 1:22

But be you doers of the word, and not hearers only, deceiving your own selves.

You must take action and utilize the knowledge to catch the fish. This means *actively* going to the best place, *actively* setting your fishing pole and placing your bait, and *actively* placing your line in the water and preparing to receive the return of fish from the *active* efforts of fishing.

Make It Personal: James 2:26

For as (Your Name)'s body without (Your Name)'s spirit is dead, so (Your Name)'s faith without (Your Name)'s works is dead also.

Bottom line: knowledge is knowledge, and it doesn't become power for you in your life, in your circumstances, and for your situations until you utilize it! You must take action!

I trust that you are beginning to clearly see just how important it is that you are reading your Bible for yourself, studying God's Word, feeding the spirit, and building a real relationship with your Creator.

When Jesus was being tested by Satan in the wilderness, Satan was quoting the Word of God with a dash of compromise and contradiction. To one who did not know the Bible for themselves, that Word may have sounded pretty accurate and trustworthy.

Needless to state, this is exactly what is happening in the church today, amongst all these different religions with all their fancy names, traditions, rules, and regulations and beautiful buildings and nice robes — which are ALL nothing more than distractions!

The Way Side

I was listening to a well-known preacher I respect, and he made a statement that stuck with me. He said, "Most Christians don't even get along; we can't even agree on something as simple and basic as salvation." Think about that; it is so sad but so true.

How easy do you think it may be to sway people in all types of directions using the Bible if the people being swayed never read it for themselves? This is exactly how Satan works right in the church, standing right behind the pulpit! Yes, even the church and a preacher can be used by Satan to <u>*Take Away*</u> your Word!

You must read, study, learn, and educate yourself in the Bible and seek God's face in worship and prayer because America, Government, Church, Jobs, President, Politicians, Preachers, Bosses, Family, Friends, Neighbors, Co-workers, Money, Houses, Cars, and Material Possessions will not suffice in the end.

You must have the eyes to see and the ears to hear, get to know who God is for yourself, and begin to build a personal one-on-one relationship and a rapport with God.

The Bible states that Jeremiah was ordained a prophet unto the nations, but what exactly has the LORD ordained you to be?

Make It Personal: Jeremiah 1:5

Before the LORD formed (Your Name) in the belly the LORD knew (Your Name); and before (Your Name) came forth out of the womb the LORD sanctified (Your Name), and the LORD ordained (Your Name) a (_____) unto the nations.

How exactly will one ever find out their ordained purpose if they do not know who God is for themselves?

We must revere God for who He is, the Creator of the Heavens and the Earth and everything within it.

God is not some magical genie in a lamp that you rub for three wishes, or some light switch that you can turn on and off as you see fit, or some mysterious Hollywood impersonator, cartoon character, or comic book hero here to entertain you and appeal to your every want and need.

This is yet another trick and TRAP of the Enemy to program you with *The Way Side* mentality that will ultimately *Take Away* from your Good Ground results!

A good life and a successful outcome always take great effort and the inner will and drive to succeed. You are what God says you are, but you can only be what you allow yourself to believe that you will be.

Hebrews 11:6

But without faith it is impossible to please [God]: for [a person] that comes to God must believe that [God] is, and that [God] is a rewarder of them that diligently seek [God].

Attempting to live a truly successful life without the power of God's Word is equivalent to trying to fill a five-gallon bucket that has seven holes drilled in the bottom — a whole lot of pointless effort with little to no beneficial outcome and results.

Keep God's seeds from falling to *The Way Side* by eliminating the opportunities for others to *Take Away* from you, and watch how quickly it will make the necessary changes that will empower you to live a better life.

CHAPTER 1 SUMMARY: MAKE IT PERSONAL

Proverbs 22:10

If _____ casts out the scorner contention shall go out; yes, strife and reproach shall cease.

John 8:31-32

Then said Jesus to _____ which believed on [Jesus], If _____ continue in [Jesus'] word, then _____ is [Jesus'] disciple indeed; and _____ shall know the truth, and the truth shall make _____ free.

John 14:6

Jesus said unto _____, [Jesus] is the way, the truth, and the life: _____ cannot come to [God the Father], but by [Jesus].

1 Peter 5:8

Be sober, be vigilant; because _____'s adversary the Devil, as a roaring lion, walks about, seeking whom he may devour.

Matthew 7:15

Beware of false prophets [false ideas, false thoughts, false feelings, false direction, false instruction] which come to _____ in sheep's clothing [looks good, sounds good, feels good, tastes good, smells good] but inwardly they are ravening wolves.

Proverbs 4:23

Keep _____'s heart with all diligence; for out of _____'s heart are the issues of life.

John 1:1-4

In the beginning was the Word, and the Word was with God, and the Word was God. The same was in the beginning with God. All things were made by [the Word]; and without [the Word] was not anything made that was made. In [the Word] was life; and the life was the light of _____.

Joshua 1:8

This book of the law shall not depart out of _____'s mouth; but _____ shalt meditate therein day and night, that _____ may observe to do according to all that is written therein: for then _____ shalt make _____'s way prosperous, and then _____ shalt have good success.

Psalm 1:2-3

But _____'s delight is in the law of the LORD; and in [the law of the LORD] does _____ meditate day and night. And _____ shall be like a tree planted by the rivers of water, that brings forth _____'s fruit in _____'s season; _____'s leaf also shall not wither; and whatsoever _____ doeth shall prosper.

James 1:22

But be you _____ a doer of the word, and not a hearer only, deceiving your own self.

James 2:26

For as _____'s body without _____'s spirit is dead, so _____'s faith without _____'s works is dead also.

Jeremiah 1:5

Before the LORD formed _____ in the belly the LORD knew _____; and before _____ came forth out of the womb the LORD sanctified _____, and the LORD ordained _____ a [_____] unto the nations.

Hebrews 11:6

But without faith it is impossible to please God: for when _____ comes to God _____ must believe that God is, and that God is a rewarder of _____ when _____ diligently seeks God.

Notes:

Good Ground: Mark 4:1-20
Chapter 2: "Stony Ground"

Parable:

Listen, behold there went out a Sower to sow: And some fell on *Stony Ground*, where it had not much earth; and immediately it sprang up, because it had no depth of earth: But when the sun was up, it was scorched; and because it had "*No Root*," it withered away.

Revelation:

The Sower soweth the Word. And these are they likewise which are sown on "Stony Ground"; who, when they have heard the word, immediately receive it with gladness: And have "*No Root*" in themselves, and so endure but for a time: afterward, when affliction of persecution ariseth for the Word's sake, immediately they are offended.

Question:

How many of you have heard something that excited you, pumped you up, motivated you, and immediately made you take action to better your life, but as soon as the first obstacle or challenge presented itself, you gave up and quit?

Never quit and never give up! If you want something, then get up and go get it!

Winners win and Losers lose!

- A *Winner* is a winner because they win and do not lose.
- A *Loser* is a loser because they lose and do not win.
- A *Quitter* is a *Loser* that decides to be a loser by quitting, thus eliminating the possibility of ever being a *Winner*.

Let that marinate, and see what reflection you see when you look into your mirror of life.

If you spend hours upon hours and days upon days investing your time and energy into planting seeds into the ground while envisioning a huge harvest to come, why would you be in agreement with someone coming right behind your hard work and efforts and digging all of those seeds up and taking away all of your hopes of receiving your harvest? Even more so, why would you go behind all your own hard work and efforts and do it to yourself?

How many times have you invested and sacrificed your time and energy into something wholeheartedly and fully motivated and pumped up, only to allow some naysayer with a pessimistic view to come burst your positive bubble of joy, and then second-guess yourself and your decisions, only to become stagnant, lacking productivity, and producing mediocre results?

Why are you allowing someone else to steal your joy and define you?

Why are you allowing someone else's opinion and judgment to outweigh your own if you know without any doubts that what you are currently doing is working for you?

Problem: "No Root"

Whether it be a personal challenge due to laziness, lack of education or experience, mediocre work ethic, and/or depreciating motivation and dedication on your part, or possibly falling into the Worldly TRAP of quick/easy money, "get rich quick" ideas, MLM Pyramid Schemes, and any other miscellaneous garbage that's thrown at you that sells you on immediate gratification without work and taking action, this also defines and represents *Stony Ground.*

Laziness is 100% unacceptable and is _not_ to be tolerated in your life or in your circle, without exception!

Laziness with an "I want something for nothing" attitude resides on *Stony Ground*, with a mentality fixated on an unearned feeling of entitlement that will only lead to destruction and chaos.

Proverbs 18:9

[A person] also that is slothful in their work is [akin] to them that is a great waster.

A lazy person is a wasteful person: a waste of talent, time, energy, and what could be, should be, and would be God's greatness!

I personally have _zero_ sympathy for *Slothfulness* and *Laziness*, nor do I cater to or support hand-outs and freebies for those who choose to go through life waiting on the rest of the world to do something for them!

You may never be able to move forward with true growth and development until you fully understand these five simple words:

No One Owes You Anything!

No matter what you may have been through and what pain, suffering, challenges, and ill feelings you may have encountered, you must come to the realization that no one in this world owes you anything.

Stop wasting your time wishing on magical stars and get up, get out, and make something great happen in your life for yourself and your family.

Your life is not a fictitious reality show or some make-believe movie on TV. No matter how great you may think you are, what pedestal you have been placed on, what accolades and accomplishments you have, you are not entitled to anything outside of what God says you are.

What do you want to be recognized as, and what legacy do you want to leave behind here on earth?

Does anyone really want to be remembered one day as a great waster and a lazy, slothful person?

Do your current actions coincide with what you want and desire?

For example:

- **You want to be wealthy.**

Okay, well, what are you currently, actively, physically doing to meet the goal?

- **You want to be healthy.**

Okay, well, what plans and criteria have you implemented to be healthy?

- **You want to be loved and appreciated.**

Okay, well, when do you put yourself to the side and go out of your way to show love and appreciation for others?

Let's see what the Bible provides as an example:

Proverbs 6:6-11

⁶ Go to the ant, thou sluggard; consider the ants ways, and be Wise:
⁷ Which having no guide, overseer, or ruler,
⁸ The ant provides meat in the summer, and the ant gathers food in the harvest.
⁹ How long will you sleep, O sluggard? When will you arise out of your sleep?
¹⁰ Yet a little sleep, a little slumber, a little folding of the hands to sleep.
¹¹ _So Shall Thy Poverty Come_ as one that travels and _So Shall Thy Want [Need or Lack] Come_ as an armed man.

Question:

When is the last time you saw an ant that was alive not actively doing something: working, moving, pulling, grabbing, or marching to the next mission?

You are being instructed to compare your hustle, your grind, your work ethic, your go-getter attitude to one of the smallest creatures on the planet!

I seriously suggest you *Man* or *Woman* up if you are willing to allow an ant to outperform you.

If you keep *"Sleeping"* on life, your success, dreams, goals, plans, growth, abundance, and prosperity will also *"Sleep"* and be nonexistent. One thing is for certain: if you *Do Nothing* and continue to *"Sleep,"* you are entitled to and guaranteed both *Poverty and Lack*, which will come to you freely and forever abide.

What is the much-needed alternative?

Solution: Find the Root

Make It Personal: John 15:5

[Jesus] is the vine, (Your Name) is the branches: If (Your Name) abides in [Jesus], and [Jesus] abides in (Your Name), (Your Name) will bring forth *Much* Fruit: for without [Jesus] (Your Name) can do *Nothing*.

There is no tree without the vine, there are no branches without the tree, and there is no fruit without the branches; there must first be the vine before there will be any successful fruit hanging from your branches.

The vine feeds, nurtures, grows, develops, and matures the branches. A branch is not a branch of its own and self-sufficient; the branch is nonexistent without the vine, and you are nonexistent without Jesus.

If you don't believe, trust, and put faith in the truth of Jesus, which is eternal, then you are making the choice to trust in the lie of this world, which is temporal. Don't expect the Jesus eternal results if you choose to have a worldly temporal mentality and mindset. You are what you eat, and you will reap exactly what you sow; what you put in is what you will get out.

Stop dreaming to the heights of Heaven with corresponding action that lies in the depths of Hell. Everybody wants, wants, wants, but hardly ever are they willing to provide the action and work ethic equivalent to that want. Talk is cheap, so if you have legs, knees, ankles, and feet, then get off your heels and start walking already! The world already provides enough excuses, so you must start digging for new treasure, and the goal is to find your own shovel.

Galatians 5:7-8

You did run well; who did hinder you that you should not obey the truth? This persuasion cometh not of him that calleth you.

Note:

I use words of encouragement and examples on a level that will resonate, but please know and understand that this verse is so much deeper than what is being conveyed at this time to make a point. If you read Chapter 5 for yourself, you will notice that in verses 7 and 8, Paul actually refers to the Law and Grace, or should I say the Law versus Grace; unfortunately, this is still a hugely misunderstood and misinterpreted subject in the church. With all its thousands of denominations teaching traditional religion with rules and regulations, people still can't seem to get it right.

[Read 2 Timothy 2:15]

For this example, to get this much-needed point across, we will apply these verses personally, without referring to the Law or Grace directly:

Make It Personal: Galatians 5:7-8

(Your Name) is doing well; who is trying to hinder (Your Name) that (Your Name) should not obey the truth? This persuasion from whoever is trying to hinder (Your Name) from obeying the truth is not of Jesus that calleth (Your Name).

Breakdown:

Anything and everything that contradicts or conflicts with the *Word* lacks *Truth*, so don't allow others to "persuade" you or "hinder" you from your calling or your truth.

Question:

What is your *Truth?*

John 14:6

[Jesus] is the **Way**, the **Truth**, and the **Life**: *No Man* cometh unto ["God" the Father], but by [Jesus].

Make It Personal: John 14:6

Jesus said unto (Your Name), [Jesus] is (Your Name)'s way, [Jesus] is (Your Name)'s truth, and [Jesus] is (Your Name)'s life: (Your Name) will not come unto the [God the Father], but by [Jesus].

Breakdown:

1. You will not come to God without Jesus.
2. Jesus is your **Way**.
3. Jesus is your **Truth**.
4. Jesus is your **Life**.

Bottom line: if it is not about Jesus, then it is about nothing. Jesus is the way, the truth, and the life; therefore, all the ifs, ands, and buts equal Jesus. Think of any positive want, need, or desire and the way to, the truth of, and the life for it equal Jesus.

Let's use Success and Prosperity:

- You want good Success and Prosperity.
- The **Way** to good Success and Prosperity = Jesus.
- The **Truth** of good Success and Prosperity = Jesus.
- The **Life** for good Success and Prosperity = Jesus.

Make It Personal:

Jesus saith unto (Your Name), you will not cometh unto the Father God and ask for Success and Prosperity but by Jesus _because_ Jesus is (Your Name)'s **Way** to Success and Prosperity, Jesus is (Your Name)'s **Truth** to Success and Prosperity, and Jesus is (Your Name)'s **Life** to Success and Prosperity.

Fill in the criteria that are most important to you:

Jesus saith unto (Your Name), you will not cometh unto the Father God and ask for (_____) but by Jesus _because_ Jesus is (Your Name)'s **Way** to (_____), Jesus is (Your Name)'s **Truth** to (_____), and Jesus is (Your Name)'s **Life** to (_____).

• Health	• Safety	• Career
• Wealth	• Wisdom	• New Job
• Financial Freedom	• Knowledge	• New Position
• Love	• Understanding	• Skill Set
• Joy	• Discernment	• Time with Family

The Bible contains very powerful information that freely provides and delivers you the keys to every door in your life, but it is up to you whether you will choose to use the keys to lock or unlock it.

Note: Jesus is the Key!

For every problem, challenge, obstacle, sickness, illness, hurt, pain, confusion, frustration, etc., Jesus is your answer!

Make It Personal: Philippians 4:13

(Your Name) can do *All Things* through [Jesus] Christ which strengtheneth (Your Name).

Do not just read the Bible like it is a bunch of old stories in some old book. You must *Make It Personal* to fully reap the rewards and find yourself within each text, so that you can maximize your personal growth and development.

When you make a choice to believe in something of value, then you will be able to respect its value rather than searching for the next quick fix that leaves you in the same exact predicament without any long-lasting or beneficial results.

How many times have we tried to do things on our own, in our own power and our own strength, only to watch it blow up in our faces and bring us back to square one, to go through the same exact trial all over again?

Philippians 3:13-14

Brethren, I count not myself to have apprehended: but this one thing I do, forgetting those things which are behind, and reaching forth unto those things which are before, I press toward the mark for the prize of the high calling of God in Christ Jesus.

Make It Personal:

One thing (Your Name) must do is forget those things which are behind in the past and reach forth unto those things which are before (Your Name) right now. (Your Name) must press forward toward the goal for (Your Name) to receive the prize of the high calling of God in Christ Jesus.

Breakdown:

We learn from the past, but we can't dwell in the past. You will never move forward in life if your thoughts have you walking in reverse. You will not climb up until you decide to stop thinking, speaking, looking, and feeling down.

You must press toward the goal, keep pushing forward for a better you, live in the now, and stay on course without letting the past hinder you from greatness.

Most importantly, never quit, never give up, and never stop trying to be the best you that you can be, by living the best life that you can live right now.

Success ultimately comes from many failures. True failure is to never try at all and experience no growth, education, or learning curve.

Note: The ultimate prize is Jesus!

Is it so hard to believe that there is a greater source outside of us and a better way in Jesus?

Matthew 28:18

All Power has been given to [Jesus] in heaven and in earth.

I guess it just comes down to what your personal definition is for "_ALL._"

If "All Power has been given to Jesus in heaven and on earth," Jesus is the "Vine," and we are the "Branches" who can do "All Things" through Jesus Christ, then why would we possess a mentality of *Stony Ground* and allow anyone or anything to steer us in another direction?

Make It Personal: 1 John 4:4

Greater is [God] that is in (Your Name) than them that are in the world.

The *Stony Ground* resembles a person who is actively in the process of improving and moving forward and then makes the decision of a Quitter to give up because of fear and opposition.

2 Corinthians 5:7

We walk by faith, not by sight.

Fear brings a person exactly what they do not want. I strongly believe that people bring it on themselves by speaking into existence the things that they do not want or need in their lives.

Proverbs 18:20-21

A person's belly shall be satisfied with the fruit of their mouth; and with the increase of their lips shall they be filled. Death and life are in the power of the tongue: and they that love it shall eat the fruit thereof.

People should put the same energy and effort they put into uniting to talk about the things they do not want and the things they do not like into uniting to speak into existence the things they do want and the things they do like.

Faith must overcome fear to allow the Power of the Kingdom to work in the earth realm!

Make It Personal: Proverbs 24:10

If (Your Name) faints in the day of adversity, (Your Name)'s strength is small.

People talk big and strong and portray this faithful character when everything is smooth sailing, going their way, but what do they do when their backs are against the wall, they are faced with opposition, their lives are threatened, their so-called faith is challenged, and they are put in life-or-death situations?

A person's truth is not revealed outside of challenge, change, and sacrifice, because strength comes only when pressure is applied. The real you is not the one you portray when all is good and everyone is cheering you on. The real you comes out when you're confronted, cussed out, ridiculed, mocked, mistreated, disrespected, tested, challenged, or taken advantage of!

How do you act when the Devil starts throwing darts in your direction (unless you are standing right next to him)?

Job 4:5

But now it is come upon you, and you faintest; it touches you, and you are troubled.

1. Do you **Faint** in the day of adversity?
2. Is your strength **Small**?
3. Are you **Troubled**?

If people invested the same energy in actually being real as they do in pretending to be, they might begin to see some positive results in their own lives for a change!

How can one portray faith when the going is good but suddenly have none when the going gets tough?

Simple! A faith faker full of fear, who never had faith to begin with, will faint in the day of adversity as soon as that Devil shows up with real situations and real life challenges. All those traditions and religious rituals come to a stop, it gets really quiet, and you can't find a penny worth of faith because they are weak and their strength is small!

You must understand this is still happening today. Even those who walked and talked with Jesus and saw the many miracles with their own eyes possessed the mentality of *Stony Ground*.

The very people who witnessed blinded eyes opened to see, deaf ears opened to hear, maimed limbs made whole, leprosy cleansed, issues of blood removed, devils cast out, sickness healed, and the dead raised to life, were the same people who by affliction of persecution allowed themselves to become offended and turned their backs on Jesus!

If those who walked and talked with Jesus faced challenges in this area, how much more do you think people may have to face and overcome it today?

We must learn to never give up, never let go of Jesus, and abide in the Word no matter what the situation or circumstances.

[Read Genesis 32: 24-30]

Jacob was left alone; and there wrestled with [Jesus] until the breaking of the day and [Jesus] said, <u>Let Me Go</u>, for the day breaketh and Jacob said, <u>I Will Not Let Thee [Jesus] Go Except Thou [Jesus] Bless Me</u> and [Jesus] Blessed Jacob there. Jacob has seen God [Jesus] face to face, and Jacob's life is preserved.

Note: Many claim that Jacob wrestled with an angel or just some random guy hanging out, but no man has seen God the Father, and there is only one who is God and Man. Therefore, this is Jesus.

[Read 2 Timothy 2:15]

For this example, we will apply this verse accordingly:

Make It Personal:

(Your Name) will not let Jesus go, except Jesus bless (Your Name).

Breakdown:

You need to grab hold of Jesus and the Word. Do not let go until you receive your blessing. Grab Jesus' ankles, put Jesus in a tough man bear hug, a cage fight chokehold or arm bar, do a figure-four wrestling maneuver, or whatever it takes. Do not give up and do not let go of Jesus until you have received your blessing!

What is it that *You* need, want, desire, or dream of achieving?

Grab hold of Jesus and make your requests known. Picture it — you have Jesus wrestled up and tied up, and Jesus is saying, "Let me go, I've got to go," but you have a strong lock on Jesus and say, "I will not let you go, Jesus, except you bless me with (fill in the blank)."

Bottom line: there is no longer any more room in your life for excuses!

As you can hopefully understand by now, there is a constant ring of the same bell. The question is, are you able to see the bell and hear the ring?

The time has come to be awakened and to eliminate the *Stony Ground* in your life.

Wake Up Your *Wisdom; Faith; Success; Finances; Growth; Healing; Goals; Joy; Peace; Happiness; Prosperity; and Abundance.*

CHAPTER 2 SUMMARY: MAKE IT PERSONAL

Proverbs 18:9

If _____ is slothful in _____'s work then _____ is [akin] to them that is a great waster.

Proverbs 6:6-11

⁶ Go to the Ant, thou Sluggard; consider the Ant's ways, and be Wise:

⁷ Which having no Guide, Overseer, or Ruler,

⁸ The Ant Provideth meat in the summer, and the Ant gathereth food in the harvest.

⁹ How long will You sleep, O Sluggard? When will You arise out of thy sleep?

¹⁰ Yet a little sleep, a little slumber, a little folding of the hands to sleep:

¹¹ <u>So Shall Thy Poverty Come</u> as one that travels and <u>So Shall Thy Want [Need or Lack] Come</u> as an armed man.

John 15:5

[Jesus] is the vine, _____ is the branches: If _____ abides in [Jesus], and [Jesus] abides in _____, _____ Will Bring Forth <u>Much</u> Fruit: for without [Jesus] _____ can do <u>Nothing</u>.

Galatians 5:7-8

_____ is doing well; who is trying to hinder _____ that _____ should not obey the truth? This persuasion from whoever is trying to hinder _____ from obeying the truth is not of Jesus that calleth _____.

John 14:6

Jesus said unto _____, [Jesus] is the way, the truth, and the life: _____ cannot come to [God the Father], but by [Jesus].

Philippians 4:13

_____ can do *All Things* through [Jesus] Christ which strengtheneth _____.

Philippians 3:13-14

One thing _____ must do is forget those things which are behind in the past, and reach forth unto those things which are before _____ Right Now. _____ must press forward toward the goal for _____ to receive the prize of the high calling of God in Christ Jesus.

Matthew 28:18

All Power has been given to [Jesus] in heaven and in earth.

1 John 4:4

Greater is God that is in _____ than them that are in the world.

2 Corinthians 5:7

_____ walks by faith, not by sight.

Proverbs 18:20-21

_____'s belly shall be satisfied with the fruit of _____'s mouth; and with the increase of _____'s lips shall _____ be filled. Death and life are in the power of _____'s tongue: and if _____ love it _____ shall eat the fruit thereof.

Proverbs 24:10

If _____ faints in the day of adversity, _____'s strength is small.

Job 4:5

But now it is come upon _____, and _____ faintest; it touches _____, and _____ is troubled.

Genesis 32:26

_____ will not let Jesus go, except Jesus bless _____.

Notes:

Good Ground: Mark 4:1-20
Chapter 3: "Thorns"

Parable:

Listen; Behold, there went out a Sower to sow: And some fell among thorns, and the thorns grew up, and choked it, and it yielded no fruit.

Revelation:

The Sower soweth the word. And these are they which are sown among thorns; such as hear the word and the cares of this world, and the deceitfulness of riches, and the lusts of other things entering in, choke the word, and it becometh unfruitful.

Question:

How many of you have heard something exciting and motivating that very well may have changed your life, but you allowed "self" and worldly distractions to get in the way, which ruined your opportunity?

One thing you must come to realize is that it's not about you, and the less focus you put on "self," the more powerful and blessed you will become.

Wisdom builds character and educates and enlightens us in the most successful ways to deal with ourselves and others.

Proverbs 3:18

Wisdom is a tree of life to them that lay hold upon Wisdom: and happy is every one that retaineth Wisdom.

Proverbs 4:7

Wisdom is the principal thing; therefore get Wisdom: and with all your getting get understanding.

Make It Personal: Proverbs 2:4,9

"*If*" (Your Name) seeks after Wisdom as (Your Name) would silver, and search for Wisdom as (Your Name) would for hidden treasures; "*Then*" (Your Name) will understand Righteousness, and Judgment, and Equity; yes, every Good Path.

- **Righteousness:** The quality of being morally right or justifiable.
- **Judgment:** The ability to make thoughtful decisions or come to sensible conclusions.
- **Equity:** The quality of being fair and impartial.

The bulk of your personal blessings from God reside in the people you bless and show God to. If you want more for yourself, then you must simply do more for others! Your true reward is helping someone else reach, obtain, or surpass their goals; in turn, you will reach, obtain, and surpass your own goals.

You can either get on God's bus of life and ride, or you can sit back with the rest of the world and watch the wheels on the bus go round and round. You are either part of the solution or part of the problem; you are either a benefit to society or a detriment.

Questions:

- What are you doing that makes a difference?
- What light in your life shines bright enough for people to see and acknowledge?
- Do you do more for others and think about others more than yourself?

- How many people have you talked to about God lately?

- Do you give God the glory, honor, and praise when the opportunity presents itself, or do you allow "self" to overshadow His accomplishments and lead the discussion?

Sadly, most people want to be blessed by God but continue to steal the praise, honor, and glory from God for the blessing once it is received.

Everything can't be I, I, I; me, me, me; my, my my; mine, mine, mine; when it's *All* His. Without Jesus, you are Nothing, and if you continue to promote self, you will reap and produce more of the same.

Bottom line: it's not about you! Never has been and never will be. The more you do for others, the more you will be blessed by God; the more you give unselfishly, the more reward you will receive spiritually from God.

A lot of times, people have the "right" ideas but the "wrong" reasons, the "right" intentions but the "wrong" motives, and the tools to get the job done "right" while actively working on the "wrong" project.

Life is a strategic game, and the world is the board. The moves (choices) you make will determine the outcome — whether you will win or lose.

Failure is *not* an option for those who choose to win. Those who make excuses choose to fail, and by choosing to fail, they also choose to lose.

Life is exactly what *you* make it. If you don't like something, then simply make the choice to change it.

The TRAP (World's System) does not want you to have a choice, have a mind of your own, think for yourself, or take control of your own life. Therefore, the TRAP provides you alternatives and lame excuses to hold on to in an attempt to justify ignorance, lack, poverty, and ultimately a life that produces very little worth, in a stagnant state of "not enough."

If you can't see or hear truth, you are a blind and deaf statistic in a TRAP society; the world does not want you to know, seek, obtain, or achieve revelation. The less you know, the less of a threat you will be. The TRAP provides distractions in the form of entertainment, so that you spend your time focused on the very things that keep you trapped, to hinder your growth and development.

Most people worship fairy tales, cartoons, and make-believe more than God and would rather be at an amusement park, on social media, watching fake "Reality" TV, playing video games, or engaging in whatever new distraction the TRAP conjures up and throws their way.

If people read the Bible, they would clearly see that most of the distractions used to destroy them are biblical principles that have been perverted and changed to achieve a specific result that ultimately steers them away from the *Truth*.

Science, movies, cartoons, comics, books, fables, video games, music, politics, inventions, ideas, concepts, and the like are all found in the Bible.

Don't fall victim to the TRAP! Everything that shines is not gold!

Distractions appear daily in many forms. You must learn how to get out of your own way and stop tripping over your own feet and creating your own challenges. The world provides enough of its own challenges to overcome on a platter, so why should you continue to add even more to your own plate unnecessarily?

Proverbs 3:5-6

Trust in the LORD with all your heart; and lean not unto your own understanding and in all your ways acknowledge the LORD, and the LORD shall direct your paths.

Psalm 37:3-5

Trust in the LORD and do good; so shalt you dwell in the land, and verily you shalt be fed.

Delight yourself also in the LORD; and the LORD shall give you the desires of your heart.

Commit your way unto the LORD; trust also in the LORD; and the LORD shall bring the desires of your heart to pass.

Jeremiah 33:2-3

Thus saith the LORD the maker thereof, the LORD that formed it, to establish it; the LORD is his name; Call unto the LORD, and the LORD will answer you, and the LORD will show you great and mighty things, which you knowest not.

You represent something one way or another: it's either God or something and someone else. We must learn to lean not unto our own understanding and simply trust God.

The farther away from God people get, the harder the lives people will have. You can't take God out of the picture, snap the shot, and then look at the picture and wonder why God isn't in the picture, then continue to do the same thing over and over every day in pertinent areas of your life. That's "insanity"!

This is exactly why there are so many failing countries, governments, churches, families, households, businesses, and schools — because of the failure to utilize knowledge and the power of unity to structure organized systems that align with biblical principles, which are the Word of God!

Make It Personal: Matthew 18:18-20

Truly Jesus says unto (Your Name), Whatsoever (Your Name) shall bind on earth shall be bound in heaven: and whatsoever (Your Name) shall loose on earth shall be loosed in heaven. Again Jesus says unto (Your Name), That if *Two* of you shall agree on earth as touching *Any Thing* that they shall ask, *It Shall Be Done For Them* of God the Father which is in heaven. For where *Two or Three* are gathered together in Jesus' name, there is Jesus in the midst of them.

The solution is to touch and agree in Jesus' name on the very problems, challenges, and shortcomings that are currently holding you back from greatness, success, abundance, prosperity, health, wealth, etc., and *It Shall Be Done For You* of God the Father which is in Heaven.

The Bible clearly states exactly how you can experience or have a personal encounter with Jesus directly. It is simply by uniting with two or three gathered together in Jesus' name, and there Jesus will be in the midst.

Don't make God and the Bible unnecessarily difficult; simply read, believe, ask, and receive!

You can't do what God can do, two is better than one, and three is greater than two. There is strength and power in unity!

We must master the art and mindset of becoming ever-learning and never allow ourselves to believe that we know it all!

John 3:10-12

Jesus answered and said unto Nicodemus, Art thou a <u>Master</u> (teacher, expert, leader, director, controller, ruler, owner, chief) of Israel, and knowest not these things? Truly, Truly, Jesus says unto thee, we speak that we do know, and testify that we have seen; and you receive not our witness. If Jesus has told you earthly things, and you believe not, how shall you believe, if Jesus tells you of heavenly things?

Breakdown:

Aren't you a master, a teacher, an expert, and a leader? And yet you don't know these basic things? We speak what we know to be true and testify of what we have seen with our own eyes, but you receive not what we know to be true or our testimony of what we have seen with our own eyes. If you can't handle milk and baby food (can't believe earthly things), then how will you handle meat (believe in heavenly things)?

Right now, I want you to use your imagination and visualize the Pharisees, Sadducees, Elders, Scribes, and Chief Priests float-walking with their expensive, fancy robes and matching hats, with the sacred scrolls of the Old Testament on their shoulders, very proud, talking highly educated, and seeming very intelligent, yet they won't listen, adhere to, or accept the very person the scrolls on their shoulders were written about.

Unfortunately, this exact thing is happening today. We know about the tool, most of us have the tool, and some carry the tool around, yet most people do not actually utilize the tool for their benefit.

Some people are so high-minded and wrapped up in themselves with their degrees, positions, accolades, and mastery that the bare-bottom basics and everyday common sense goes right over their heads.

Do not allow the "Thorns" of this world to choke your word and make you unfruitful!

Do not mimic the behaviors and follow the detrimental examples of the Pharisees, Sadducees, Elders, Scribes, and Chief Priests!

Proverbs 28:19

A person that follows after vain people shall have poverty enough.

Proverbs 12:11

A person that follows vain people is void of understanding.

Vain:

Producing no result and no purpose; useless, pointless, hopeless; ineffective, fruitless, profitless, unrewarding, unproductive, unsuccessful.

Make It Personal:

If (Your Name) follows after ineffective, unproductive, unsuccessful people with no purpose, then (Your Name) is void of understanding and (Your Name) shall have poverty enough.

I absolutely love the Bible! How much more simplistic can it get?

Basically, you can't follow stupid and get smart. You can't follow a Loser and be a Winner. You can't follow the broke and become wealthy. A fruitless person does not possess any beneficial fruit, and an unrewarding person has no intentions of rewarding you!

The "poverty enough" is a biblical guarantee for those who decide to follow people who reside, set up camp, and choose to dwell in the land of the vain!

Notice, the Bible never states that the vain people are void of understanding or will have poverty enough. It only specifies these results for those who make a choice to *follow after* the vain people.

Please understand that everyone does not have your best interest in mind. Most people only want to get and take from you, with no intentions of you benefiting in any way. If that is too difficult for you to believe, then I'm not sure what world you are currently living in, and I strongly suggest that you wake up, open your eyes to see, and open your ears to hear!

Be very careful who you follow and eliminate the "Thorns" in your life by connecting to your Creator, who is the true source.

It is no secret that the enemy is crafty and aware of your weaknesses. He knows exactly what it takes to provide you with the choices and opportunities to be unfruitful, but ultimately, he only has the power that you allow him to have.

A lot of things are presented with innocence and appear harmless to the natural eye, but the motivation and preparation taking place behind the scenes is detrimental to your success. This is yet another reason why you must make it a priority to know who God is for yourself.

Ephesians 6:11-13

Put on the whole armor of God that you may be able to stand against the schemes and tricks of the Devil. For we wrestle not against flesh and blood, but against principalities, against powers, against the rulers of the darkness of this world, against spiritual wickedness in high places. Wherefore take unto you the whole armor of God that you may be able to withstand in the evil day, and having done all, to stand.

Put on the Whole Armor of God:

- Loins girt with **Truth**
- Breastplate of **Righteousness**
- Feet shod with preparation of the gospel of **Peace**
- Above all, the shield of **Faith**
- Helmet of **Salvation**
- Sword of the Spirit, which is the **Word of God**

Imagine a spy going on a secret mission to obtain information without being seen, but he is wearing a bright orange shirt with a clashing yellow hat and lime green light-up shoes.

Imagine a soldier dressed in fatigues with no boots on their feet, heading into a heated battle with no weapon or ammo.

Imagine a quarterback weighing 150 pounds, playing on the field on national TV with no helmet or pads for protection, with the weakest offensive line in history.

These things are detrimental and conflict with success, but living in this world without the Armor of God is far worse than all three combined.

Without armor and without protection, you are the easiest target to overcome and to take advantage of. Think of anything of importance to you. In some way, shape, form, or fashion, you are actively doing something to armor it. Is it not wise to do the same thing with the most important aspects of your life?

What sense does it make to work hard every day to obtain, yet not put the same energy and thought into armoring that which was obtained? When you obtain success, health, wealth, abundance, prosperity, love, joy, peace, and happiness, what are you going to do to protect it and keep it from the "Thorns" of life?

Make It Personal: Exodus 14:13-14

Fear not (Your Name), stand still (Your Name), see the salvation of the LORD (Your Name), hold your peace (Your Name); the LORD shall fight for (Your Name).

Make It Personal: Psalm 23:1

The LORD is (Your Name's) shepherd; (Your Name) shall not want, need, or lack.

Make It Personal: Psalm 18:2

The LORD is (Your Name's) rock, and (Your Name)'s fortress, and (Your Name)'s deliverer; (Your Name)'s God, (Your Name)'s strength, in whom (Your Name) will trust.

Romans 8:18

For I reckon that the sufferings of this present time are not worthy to be compared with the glory which shall be revealed in us.

Personal Tangent:

"I may tolerate a little stupidity and ignorance to gain a whole lot of wisdom and knowledge, and I may be a target of the Devil's tricks to be a conqueror with God's blessings. Society may be the walking dead full of the blind and deaf, but my God provides me with the eyes to see and ears to hear. I may experience backbiting, talebearing, gossip, envy, hate, and jealousy, but God continues to allow me to overcome and gives them more and more to talk about by providing me with power, wisdom, truth, abundance, and prosperity. The negativity of the world may be arrogance and boasting, but the positivity I possess is humility and meekness. I may tolerate a man's hate to gain God's love, and I will entertain the <u>sufferings</u> of Earth to reach the <u>glory</u> of Heaven."

The negatives will never outweigh the positives, as God is the Creator of both; the created will never defeat the Creator.

A person must stand for something, or they will fall for anything!

Who are you, and what do you stand for?

When the Devil hears your name, does he become uneasy and cringe, does he laugh uncontrollably, or, even worse, does he do nothing because he doesn't even know who you are?

What challenges, changes, and sacrifices are you willing to make to reach, obtain, and surpass your goals, to ultimately live in a state of "More Than Enough" with true success?

Life is not a Hollywood movie, a fictitious "Reality" show on TV, or a video game or social media experience!

Proverbs 23:12

Apply your heart unto instruction, and your ears to the words of knowledge.

Question:

If I told you that it was raining money outside, would you immediately pick up the phone and call everyone you know to relay the info, or would you first look out your door or window to see for yourself if it's even true?

Using this same highly unlikely analogy, why do people accept anything and everything that is given as a truth without doing their own due diligence and making it a priority to be in the know?

I assure you that over 50% of what you have been told, taught, and subjected to is 100% purposely falsified and inaccurate info!

Of course, most people assume that everything is done with their best interest in mind, but this could not be further from the truth. The more ignorant you are, the less of a threat you are, and the more they will utilize and take advantage of you as they see fit. If you won't just take my word that it's raining money outside, then why should you just take any other info thrown at you — seriously, what's the difference?

You have been lied to since the very first breath you breathed, and you have been a willing and able participant unknowingly promoting these lies all your life!

The world, the government, politicians, preachers, teachers, family, friends, neighbors, religion, tradition, and history books all lie, and it's up to you to decipher what's real from what's fake!

If you are not going through any transitions in your life, everything is always great, everyone loves you and gets along with you, and you face no opposition or challenges, then I strongly suggest you take a long, hard look in the mirror, because you, respectfully, are no threat.

Why do you think mentality and mindset, eyes to see, and ears to hear are so important?

You must apply yourself and take your life back into your own hands, away from the TRAP System: a system of confinement, imprisonment, and captivity, which is ultimately slavery! Everything that looks, sounds, smells, tastes, and feels good is not necessarily good for you. The TRAP has a way to appeal to your emotions that is ultimately detrimental to your wellbeing.

Most marketing and advertising is basically a psychological hustle to make you want more of what everyone else has and convince you to do what everyone else is doing. Whether the outcome hurts you and your family or not, it doesn't matter to them; only right here and right now matters to them because they have already created the solution to your future problem, which they purposely created so you would need the future solution!

Most (if not all) of what you are allowed to see is purposely shoved down your throat so you remain a non-threat to the agenda, and sadly, most of it is fictitious, fake, fraudulent, and phony. But people taste, chew, and swallow it up and make it their truth, just as planned.

The more distracted you are chasing after the next new thing, trying to be actors and actresses, desiring and envying what you see on TV and in music videos, trying to keep up with the world, the more TRAPPED you allow yourself and your family to become!

We must pay attention to and beware of the schemes and tricks and worldly seeds that are being planted in our lives daily to purposely cause death and destruction. What you may think is cute, funny, and innocent now will be the exact same things that cause ruin and havoc in your life in the future. The things that are supposedly implemented for our convenience are the very things that are destroying us and tearing us apart, little by little, every day.

We all know that technology is great, but the further it advances, the more we as people grow apart from one another, because technology steals away our humanity. How many of us are guilty of having a one-hour text-a-thon with correspondence that could have and probably should have been communicated directly, which may have taken all of five minutes?

We live in a world now where people will attempt to find someone on social media rather than getting up off their shoulders and heels and simply talking to the person sitting right across from them; relationships and even marriages are created online rather than in person, and people seem more interested in living their lives through social media and technological platforms rather than directly interacting with one another. This is very dangerous and detrimental behavior that encourages division and separation and brings discord and strife, preventing the growth and development of traits that contribute to unity and harmony amongst the people.

These are the types of things that are usually overlooked because most people would consider them harmless. They don't understand that these very things contribute to separation, which makes us unfruitful.

Proverbs 22:5

Thorns and snares are in the way of the froward: a person that doth keep their soul shall be far from them.

Breakdown:

Thorns and traps are in the way of the people who are difficult to deal with: a person who keeps their soul shall be far from the Thorns and traps and those who are difficult to deal with.

Thorns and traps come in all forms: people, materials, entertainment, work, rules, regulations, traditions, religion, and any other growth-hindering distractions that keep you from living in a state of More Than Enough!

Are Thorns and traps in your way? If so, what exactly are you prepared to do about it?

Unfortunately, on most occasions, the Thorns and traps are set by the ones who are the closest to you — those who are supposed to love you, be there for you, and look out for you, rather than consistently installing roadblocks and detours to your success.

Make It Personal: Matthew 10:36

(Your Name)'s foes shall be they of (Your Name)'s own household.

Hate, envy, and jealousy with a side of gossip, talebearing, and backbiting is an evil and wicked contributing factor that causes unnecessary discord and strife in one's life!

This is yet another form of our seeds being choked by the *Thorns* and distractions of life.

It amazes me that the majority will invest more time and energy into taking offense rather than using that same exact time and energy to implement the necessary changes that will empower them to be a better person and a positive contributing factor to a dying society.

Bottom line, a person who can be bought is nothing more than a slave, even if they are being provided a fictitious façade of imaginary freedom which is non-existent without Jesus.

Make It Personal: John 8:36

If the Son therefore shall make (Your Name) free, (Your Name) shall be free indeed.

Does Wisdom and Knowledge fall on "Good Ground" in your life or are you full of Excuses and *Thorns*?

Notes:

_____
_____
_____
_____
_____
_____
_____
_____
_____

CHAPTER 3 SUMMARY: MAKE IT PERSONAL

Proverbs 3:18

Wisdom is a tree of life to _____
if _____ lay hold upon
Wisdom: and happy is _____
if _____ retains Wisdom.

Proverbs 4:7

Wisdom is the principal thing; therefore _____
get Wisdom: and with all _____'s getting
_____ get understanding.

Proverbs 2:4,9

"*If* _____ seeks after Wisdom as
_____ would silver, and search for
Wisdom as _____ would for hidden
treasures; "*Then*" _____ will understand
Righteousness, and Judgment, and Equity; yes Every <u>Good</u>
Path.

Proverbs 3:5-6

Trust in the LORD with all _____'s
heart; and lean not unto _____'s
understanding and in all _____'s
ways acknowledge the LORD, and the LORD shall direct
_____'s paths.

Psalm 37:3-5

_____ trust in the LORD,
and _____ do good; so
shalt _____ dwell in the land,
and verily _____ shalt be fed.

_____ delight yourself also in the LORD; and the LORD shall give _____ the desires of _____'s heart. _____ commit your way unto the LORD; _____ trust also in the LORD; and the LORD shall bring the desires of _____'s heart to pass.

Jeremiah 33:2-3

Thus saith the LORD the maker thereof, the LORD that formed it, to establish it; the LORD is his name; _____ call unto the LORD, and the LORD will answer _____, and the LORD will show _____ great and mighty things, which _____ knowest not.

Matthew 18:18-20

Truly Jesus says unto _____, Whatsoever _____ shall bind on earth shall be bound in heaven: and whatsoever _____ shall loose on earth shall be loosed in heaven. Again Jesus says unto _____ That if *Two* of you shall agree on earth as touching *Any Thing* that they shall ask, *It Shall Be Done For Them* of God the Father which is in heaven. For where *Two or Three* are gathered together in *Jesus*' name, there is *Jesus* in the midst of them.

Proverbs 28:19

If _____ follows after vain people _____ shall have poverty enough.

Proverbs 12:11

If _____ follows vain people _____ is void of understanding.

Ephesians 6:11-13

Put on the whole armor of God _____ that you may be able to stand against the schemes and tricks of the Devil. _____ wrestles not against flesh and blood, but against principalities, against powers, against the rulers of the darkness of this world, against spiritual wickedness in high places. Wherefore take unto you _____ the whole armor of God that you may be able to withstand in the evil day, and having done all, to stand.

Exodus 14:13-14

Fear not _____, stand still _____, see the salvation of the LORD _____, hold your peace _____; the LORD shall fight for _____.

Psalm 23:1

The LORD is _____'s shepherd; _____ shall not want, need, or lack.

Psalm 18:2

The LORD is _____'s rock, and _____'s fortress, and _____'s deliverer; _____'s God, _____'s strength, in whom _____ will trust.

Romans 8:18

For _____ reckon that the sufferings of this present time are not worthy to be compared with the glory which shall be revealed in _____.

Proverbs 23:12

Apply _____'s heart unto instruction, and _____'s ears to the words of knowledge.

Proverbs 22:5

If _____ keeps _____'s soul, _____ shall be far from the Thorns and Traps in the way and of those who are difficult to deal with.

Matthew 10:36

_____'s foes shall be they of _____'s own household.

John 8:36

If the Son therefore shall make _____ free, _____ shall be free indeed.

Notes:

Good Ground: Mark 4:1-25
Chapter 4: "Good Ground"

Parable:

Listen; Behold, there went out a Sower to sow: And other fell on "Good Ground," and did yield fruit that sprang up and increased; and brought forth, some thirty, and some sixty, and some hundred.

Revelation:

The Sower soweth the word. And these are they which are sown on "Good Ground"; such as *Hear* the word, and *Receive* the word, and *Bring Forth* fruit, some thirtyfold, some sixty, and hundred.

Defining Thirtyfold, Sixtyfold, Hundredfold:

Being 30, 60, or 100 times as large, as great, or as many as some understood size, degree, amount, or quantity of increase.

Question:

How many of you have heard something that excited you, pumped you up, motivated you, and immediately took action to improve something for the better in your life; you ignored the voice or thought of opposition and negativity (The Way Side); you did not give up or quit due to an obstacle or challenge (Stony Ground); you stayed focused on the goal without giving in to distractions (Thorns); and you *Hear* the word, *Receive* the word, and consistently *Bring Forth* and *Produce* thirty, sixty, or one-hundred fold (Good Ground)?

> Where is your mentality and mindset right now?
> How do you currently think and react in life situations?
> Which one of these four mirrors is a true reflection of you today?

Does the message of "Good Ground" provide you with the vision and fall upon open eyes that are willing to see change and growth, or does the message fall upon deaf ears attached to a hard head, with a mentality and mindset that "brings forth or produces" little to nothing?

Do you have Ears to Hear the wisdom and knowledge that may allow you to ultimately change your life and circumstances?

Imagine if your wisdom and knowledge, faith and favor, health and wealth, income and finances, and abundance and prosperity were 30, 60, or 100 times greater!

Some type of seed is sown daily. The question you must ask yourself is: what kind of seeds do you allow to take root in your life? Are the positive and beneficial seeds falling into Good Ground?

All your focus needs to be on the Good Ground because it's the Good Ground that provides you with a Great Harvest.

What is the Good Ground, and how do we focus on it to obtain the Great Harvest?

The most simplistic answer: the Good Ground is the Source that provides the Great Harvest, and it is our duty to understand the Source to enjoy the benefits of the harvest.

How do we understand the Source? _Wisdom!_

Proverbs 4:7

Wisdom is the principal thing; Therefore get wisdom: And in all your getting, get understanding.

How do we get wisdom?

Proverbs 9:10

The fear of the LORD is the beginning of wisdom: and the knowledge of the holy is understanding.

Wisdom in ALL things begins with the fear, reverence, and respect of the LORD in whom is the True Source of ALL things righteous.

Remember, God is a loving God, so this fear is not the natural fear of being scared or afraid but that of reverence and respect.

Make It Personal: 2 Timothy 1:7

For God has not given (Your Name) the spirit of fear, but of power and of love and of a sound mind.

Now, how do we benefit from having reverence for the LORD?

Proverbs 3:5-6

Trust in the LORD with all your heart; and lean not unto your own understanding.

In all your ways acknowledge the LORD, and the LORD shall direct your paths.

Make It Personal: Proverbs 16:3

If (Your Name) commits (Your Name)'s works unto the LORD, then (Your Name)'s thoughts shall be established.

How do we commit our works unto the LORD?

First and foremost, you must know who you are, who you belong to, and what you stand for. This will enable you to make sure that seeds are falling onto Good Ground in your life, rather than the negative alternatives that are not productive or beneficial for you or your family.

Right now, you may experience a shift as you continue to read because we are entering the most important aspects of the ground in which your seeds reside. Up to this point, I have appealed more to the natural. This is by design, so that you have a full understanding of the importance of how you allow the seeds to fall.

If we are all honest with ourselves, there are certain questions we ask that we sincerely need answers to, but there never seems to be an answer that resonates with us. This is mainly because we are asking what seems to be the right people (who have the wrong motives) and/or we are asking the wrong people (who may have the right motives but simply lack the knowledge and understanding to be helpful).

At one point or another (past, present, and/or future), we have asked or we will ask ourselves these questions:

1. Who am I?
2. Where did I come from?
3. Why am I here?

How can you truly understand what, when, where, how, and why if you don't know who?

It is impossible to obtain the Good Ground and the Great Harvest if you do not know who you are!

The Way Side, Stony Ground, and Thorns are the only options available to you until you know who you really are. All success is not good success. The World's System promotes the image of prosperity, but it is only detrimental to you if you never truly prosper. You can have everything in this world, but if you don't know who you are, you are broken. The lie will never outweigh your truth, and your light will always outshine the darkness.

This information is pertinent to your elevation, growth, and development. It is imperative that you have the full wisdom, knowledge, and understanding of who you are.

Hold onto this book tightly, keep reading, and don't let it go. Truth has a way of pulling us onto an emotional rollercoaster, especially when it is foreign to us.

John 4:24

God is a Spirit: and they that worship God must worship God in spirit and in truth.

Genesis 1:26

And God said, Let us make man in our image, after our likeness.

God is a Spirit, and you are made in the image and after the likeness of God, which means you too are a spirit being, not the flesh and blood you see when you look in the mirror. You do not have a spirit; you are a spirit that has a body. Please do not get this confused with the Holy Spirit (Capital S); I am referring to you individually. You are a spirit (lowercase s) made in the image and likeness of God, which is why they who worship God must worship in spirit (lowercase s) and in truth.

The only way to worship God is in spirit (the real you, not what you see in the mirror) and in truth, and the only way you can do this is by knowing who you really are and knowing who and what the truth is. A person in the natural out of their flesh and blood who does not know who they really are does not know the truth, and if they don't know their own truth, it's a strong possibility that they don't know who the truth is either.

Make It Personal: John 14:6

Jesus saith unto (Your Name), Jesus is the way, the truth, and the life: (Your Name) cannot come unto the Father [God], but by Jesus.

The only way to worship God is by knowing who and what you really are, which is a spirit, and knowing the truth, which is Jesus. Outside of these two biblical requirements, there is no way to truly worship God. It is in your best interest as a spirit (lowercase s) to allow the Holy Spirit (Capital S) to make intercession for you so that you can successfully communicate with God in His will.

Make It Personal: Romans 8:26-27

Likewise the Spirit also helps (Your Name)'s infirmities: for (Your Name) knows not what (Your Name) should pray for as (Your Name) ought: but the Spirit itself makes intercession for (Your Name) with groanings which cannot be uttered. And [God the Father] that searches the hearts knows what is the mind of the [Holy] Spirit, because the [Holy] Spirit makes intercession for (Your Name) according to the will of God.

As simplistic a subject as prayer is, there is still so much unnecessary confusion, so let me share with you exactly what I do for clarification: I in spirit pray to the Father God in Heaven in, by, and through Jesus the Christ, with the guidance of the Holy Spirit.

I am praying to the Father, which is permitted, accessible, and authorized by the one and only name above every name with all power in Heaven and in Earth, which is Jesus, with the intercession, guidance, and assistance of the Holy Spirit. I strongly believe that acknowledging the Unity of the Father, Son, and Spirit, following biblically stated direction and instruction, empowers the prayer and the building of a relationship through prayer.

Now let's get back to who you are.

Genesis 1:27

So God created man in his own image, in the image of God created he him; male and female created he them.

Genesis 2:7

And the LORD God formed man of the dust of the ground, and breathed into his nostrils the breath of life; and man became a living soul.

Notice that God created man in Chapter 1 of Genesis but did not form him until Chapter 2. This is because the Spiritual always goes before the Natural. We in the Natural World, which is seen, are always playing catch-up with the Spiritual World, which is unseen. Simply put, you existed as a spirit in the spirit realm before you were born into the natural.

Make It Personal: Jeremiah 1:5

Before God formed (Your Name) in the belly God knew (Your Name); and before (Your Name) came forth out of the womb God sanctified (Your Name) and God ordained (Your Name) to be a (fill in the blank) unto the nations.

Just like Adam is a spirit created in the image of God in Chapter 1 of Genesis _Before_ he is formed in Chapter 2 of Genesis, and just like Jeremiah is a spirit known, sanctified, and ordained by God _Before_ he is formed, you too are a spirit that existed _Before_ you entered the womb; you were here _Before_ you were here.

Be very careful not to allow those who have ulterior motives and simply want to control you to steer you into the religious traditions of men attempting to tell you who you are and God's will (as if they know) for your life.

Isaiah 55:8-9

For God's thoughts are not your thoughts, neither are your ways God's ways, saith the LORD.

For as the heavens are higher than the earth, so are God's ways higher than your ways, and God's thoughts than your thoughts.

You are a spirit who comes from God and is created by God, placed here on Earth to fulfill <u>Kingdom Purpose</u>, to be a representation and reflection of the <u>Kingdom</u>. You have been ordained and sanctified to use your God-Given Gift to Seek and to Save that which is lost and bring them back home.

Please read that paragraph again and again and again, until it awakens something on the inside of you. You will never penetrate and maximize the Good Ground until you fully understand your purpose, and you will not understand purpose until you know exactly who you are.

You, as a speaking spirit, have been given the power, authority, and dominion as a child of the living God to be a joint heir, a citizen, an ambassador, and most importantly, a servant to the *King*.

Make It Personal: Genesis 1:26,28

And God said, let (Your Name) have dominion over the fish of the sea, and over the fowl of the air, and over the cattle, and over all the earth, and over every creeping thing that creeps upon the earth.

And God blessed (Your Name), and God said unto (Your Name), Be fruitful, and multiply, and replenish the earth, and subdue it: and have dominion over the fish of the sea, and over the fowl of the air, and over every living thing that moves upon the earth.

You must fully understand the Good Ground so that you are able to eliminate the Way Side, Stony Ground, and Thorns for yourself and others.

There is a reason that the powers that be, including the government and even religious organizations with all their denominations, distractions, confusion, rules, regulations, and traditions of men, do not promote, preach, or teach the God of the Bible, who you really are, and the power you possess. This is because it will eliminate their position and the control they have and so desperately want to keep over you and your family.

Remember, religious leaders who did not want to lose their positions with the government and the people were the very ones who plotted, planned, and ultimately had Jesus crucified. Blinded by selfishness, greed, religion, tradition, rules, and regulations, they did not have the eyes to see that the scrolls they walked around with were written of the very man that they were envious, jealous, and hateful of, even unto death.

2 Timothy 2:15

Study to show yourself approved unto God, a workman that needs not to be ashamed, rightly dividing the word of truth.

I cannot express deeply enough in mere words how vitally important it is that you are reading your Bible for yourself and building a relationship with God for yourself, so that you are able to hear directly from God for yourself.

I will boldly tell you what most will not: Man is *not* your teacher!

There is only one teacher for the spirit, and anything and everything that is spiritually taught comes from one teacher. Yes, revelation and confirmation come through Man, but only one teacher is supposed to be speaking through or utilizing the Man for the Glory of God.

John 14:26

But the Comforter, which is the Holy Ghost, whom the Father will send in Jesus' name, the Holy Ghost shall teach you ALL Things, and bring ALL Things to your remembrance, whatsoever Jesus has said unto you.

1 John 2:27

But the anointing which you have received of God [in, by, and through Jesus] abides in you, and you need not that any man teach you: but as the same anointing teach you of all things, and is truth, and is no lie, and even as it has taught you, you shall abide in God [in, by, and through Jesus].

Disregard all the self-proclaimed titles and the worldly man-made accolades, which outside of God mean absolutely nothing anyway. Don't be impressed by the shiny, fancy robes (things of this world) and the eloquent speech of Man, for without God we are *Nothing*!

Make It Personal: 1 John 4:4

You are of God, (Your Name), and have overcome [the enemy and the opposition]: because greater is God that is within (Your Name), than [the enemy and opposition] that is in the world.

Make It Personal: Philippians 4:13

(Your Name) can do ALL Things through Christ which strengthens (Your Name).

Make It Personal: Psalm 23:1

The LORD is (Your Name)'s shepherd: (Your Name) shall not want [need or lack].

This is the mindset and mentality we must possess, with a clear understanding of how to move forward to fulfill our specific purpose.

Romans 12:2

And be not conformed to this world: but be you transformed by the renewing of your mind, that you may prove what is that good, and acceptable, and perfect, will of God.

The renewing of our minds from the World's System and transitioning ourselves back to the original intent is the deadliest weapon to the enemy and opposition because it aligns us to be able to see our true identity and purpose.

Make It Personal: John 17:14

Jesus has given (Your Name) God's Word; and the world [and the system of the world] has hated (Your Name), because (Your Name) is not of the world [and the system of the world], even as Jesus is not of the world [and the system of the world].

We are in this World System, but we are not of this system, and our purpose and identity cannot and will not be discovered in a foreign system where most of us reside but do not belong.

Do you not look around and see some type of religion, church building, or group function on every other corner?

How is it that the world is in so much turmoil with all this so called "good" and "great" opportunity around us?

Why are so many Christians; Catholics; Muslims; Buddhists; Hinduists; Scientologists; Mormons; 7th Day Adventists; Latter Day Saints; Rastafarians; Black Israelites; Jehovah's Witnesses; devil worshippers; sorcerers; warlocks; witches; sun, moon, and star worshippers; animal and statue worshippers; atheists; apostles; prophets; preachers; pastors; deacons; ministers; bishops; priests; rabbis; world leaders; governments; politicians; bankers; Black Panthers; White Supremacists; and mafia, cartel, street gangs, Ku Klux Klan, and Black Lives Matter members sad and broken, with apparently no resolution for improvement?

Hosea 4:6

My people are destroyed for lack of knowledge.

People seek and search to fill a void on the inside but have not come to the realization that what they are seeking and searching for will never be found outside of themselves. Nothing in this world or of this world will ever empower you to fulfill your purpose.

We live in a very fictitious world, where we make even our reality fake. We now call what is wrong right and what is right wrong, and sense is no longer common for the majority. We are enslaved and destroyed by our lack of knowledge, our failure to know who we are, and our lack of understanding the assigned purpose we are here to fulfill.

God the Father, Jesus Christ the Son of God, and the Holy Spirit are _not_ a religion, _not_ some fictional characters, and the Bible is _not_ some story book written to entertain you, nor was it written to enslave you or control you.

Unfortunately, every lie has some truth, and all evil has hints of good, which is why it is so easy to confuse, deceive, and manipulate people. The Enemy and the Opposition take from the Original, distort it to fit their narrative and agenda, and then package it up and sell it to you as the truth.

How many verses and quotes in the Bible are preached and taught in error, misleading and confusing the people with misinterpretations, purposeful falsehoods, and misquotes that empower contradictions, and/or adding and taking away to fit a specific message or agenda?

The World's System is designed to promote thoughts and ideas that hinder you, which is detrimental to the Good Ground in your life by persistently and consistently advertising, promoting, and ultimately enabling the opposition: the Way Side, Stony Ground, and Thorns.

Okay, hold on tightly to the book again....

Satan the Devil, who is the Enemy and the Opposition, knows more biblical word and understands the Power of Unity more than most so-called followers of the Bible do! This is unfortunately an undeniable, undisputable fact.

Devil worshippers, mafias, cartels, street gangs, secret societies, culture-driven supremacist groups, and even something as simple as the military or a sports organization have more unity within them then any church or religious organization; unbeknownst to most, all these groups (including devil worshippers) use biblical principles to thrive.

The Enemy is _not_ an originator of anything. Everything, and I mean everything, he does is stolen from the Creator of Heaven and Earth, which is the God of the Bible, and then perverted to accomplish whatever the agenda may be.

The Devil has no inventions, new tricks, or original plans or ideas; he was created by the same Creator who created us. The created will never outweigh or outperform the Creator!

God is Almighty and All Powerful; nothing is before and nothing will be after. God is the Alpha and the Omega, the beginning and the end, and God is the *Source* of _all_ things.

When you begin to realize and know who you really are, you understand that there is only one true source, and the power you initially received (as the original intent) from the source is to have authority and dominion in the Earth as a reflection and representation of our Father God in Heaven.

In the garden, Adam and Eve (by their disobedience of the instruction and direction given by God not to eat of the Tree of Good and Evil) gave away their God-given power, authority, and dominion to the Enemy because they placed their faith and belief in the word of the serpent over the Word of God.

Yes, I am telling you that Adam and Eve put their faith in the word of the serpent over the Word of God.

Here is another biblical truth most so-called followers of the Bible clearly do not fully understand. Every time they use the word "faith," they consider it only a positive and consider it Godly; however, this could not be further from the truth.

I had no intention of going into depth on the word "faith" in this book, but I trust you will agree to entertain this brief tangent for clarification regarding my statement about Adam and Eve.

Word of God: Genesis 2:16-17

And the LORD God commanded Adam, saying, Of every tree of the garden you may freely eat: But of the tree of the knowledge of good and evil, you shalt not eat of it: for in the day that you eat thereof you shalt surely die.

Faith in the Word of God: Genesis 2:2-3

And Eve said unto the serpent, We may eat of the fruit of the trees of the garden: But of the fruit of the tree which is in the midst of the garden, God has said, You shall not eat of it, neither shall you touch it, lest you die.

Word of the Serpent Contradicting God's Word: Genesis 2:4-5

And the serpent said unto Eve, You shall not surely die: For God does know that in the day you eat thereof, then your eyes shall be opened, and you shall be as gods, knowing good and evil.

Faith in the Word of the Serpent: Genesis 2:6

And when Eve saw that the tree was good for food, and that it was pleasant to the eyes, and a tree to be desired to make one wise, she took of the fruit thereof, and did eat, and gave also unto Adam with Eve; and Adam did eat.

So here we have the Word of God and a commandment not to eat of the fruit of the Tree of Good and Evil. Eve is fully aware, and initially her faith is in the Word of God, as she explains to the serpent. However, the serpent provides Eve with a new contradicting word, and then Eve makes a choice to disobey the Word of God that she clearly understood and put her faith in the word of the Serpent.

Biblical Definition of Faith: Hebrews 11:1

Now faith is the substance of things hoped for, the evidence of things not seen.

As you can clearly read, nowhere does this definition specifically support a positive or negative connotation, which means that faith can be for a positive and faith can be for a negative, interchangeably.

So, what was the substance of things hoped for, and the evidence of things not seen for Adam and Eve?

- Eyes shall be opened
- Shall be as gods
- Know good and evil
- To make one wise

Substance of things hoped for and evidence of things not seen is in the God-given heart/mind/choice of the individual, which is why I personally feel that Romans 10:17 is one of the most misquoted, misinterpreted, and misunderstood verses in the Bible.

Misunderstood Definition of Faith for Most: Romans 10:17

So then faith comes by hearing, and hearing by the word of God.

Breakdown:

So then faith comes by hearing.

The message we need to understand is the clear statement that faith comes by hearing. This makes perfect sense because we cannot put our faith into something unless we have heard about it.

So now if faith comes by hearing, the question is: faith in what and hearing what?

The latter part of the verse answers this question: "hearing by the word of God."

As I mentioned previously, we don't add, and we don't take away. However, we do receive and accept revelation, which encourages wisdom, knowledge, and understanding to empower and enable basic comprehension.

Question: Faith in what?
Answer: The Word of God.

Breakdown: So then faith [in the Word of God] comes by hearing, and hearing by the Word of God.

Question: Hearing what?
Answer: The Word of God.

Revelation: So then faith [in the Word of God] comes by hearing [the Word of God].

As much as people would love to argue and find all the reasons why this is not exactly what this verse means, it is simplistic. This verse shoots holes in their denominations and their man-made messages because now they can no longer see faith only in a positive light, as people may choose to put their faith in a lie.

Think about it:

- Does a devil worshipper have faith in the Devil?
- Do children have faith in Santa Claus?

Breakdown:

- So then faith [in devil worshipping] comes by hearing [about devil worshipping].
- So then faith [in Santa Claus] comes by hearing [about Santa Claus].

Now ask yourself, does either of the examples I just provided have anything to do with the Word of God? No, absolutely nothing!

- Devil worshippers putting their faith in the Devil is real and true but has nothing to do with hearing the Word of God.
- Children putting their faith in Santa Claus, who is a man-made lie, has nothing to do with hearing the Word of God.

The most important part of the verse is the most overlooked: <u>*Faith Comes by Hearing!*</u>

Eve told the serpent about her faith in what God said because, at one point or another, she heard it. The same goes for the faith she put in the word of the serpent after she heard it.

If you read the account in its entirety, you will realize the following:

- Adam and Eve put their faith in the Word of God.
- Eve put her faith in the contradicting word of the serpent over the Word of God and the word of her husband.
- Adam put his faith in the contradicting word of the serpent and the word of his wife over the Word of God.

To not have a clear understanding of faith, and even more so the Kingdom, is yet another prime example of being trapped in The Way Side, Stony Ground, and Thorns, which keep you as far away from the Good Ground as possible.

Allow God to lead you and guide you by way of the Holy Spirit to give you the Eyes to See and the Ears to Hear. Stop depending on man and stop looking to a third party to rightly divide the word of Truth for you.

The Word of God is alive, and it never fails. For every situation, circumstance, and/or challenge that you may face, I assure you that the Word of God has the answers and the solutions.

God speaks to us in the most simplistic ways, so if you are looking for thunder, lightning, and earthquakes, you may completely miss it.

God speaks to us directly through the Holy Spirit. If it involves other people, it is usually by way of confirmation and revelation. A person either reveals something new that is then confirmed or confirms what has already been revealed.

God will not contradict His own word, and He will not send someone to you who will contradict His word, either. If God is speaking, it will always line up with His own word. It will usually be something you don't want to hear or do, and more than likely, it benefits someone else and not yourself.

Seeds must be placed in the Good Ground, so you must eliminate The Way Side, Stony Ground, and Thorns in your life. Be very careful not to let those who reside in these three areas manipulate you with vain words and babbling, which threaten the Good Ground.

In the beginning of the chapter, I provided you with the following definition:

Defining Thirtyfold, Sixtyfold, Hundredfold:

Being 30, 60, or 100 times as large, as great, or as many as some understood size, degree, amount, or quantity of increase.

I also provided you with the following statement:

Imagine if your wisdom and knowledge, faith and favor, health and wealth, income and finances, and abundance and prosperity were 30, 60, or 100 times greater!

Now, this sounds great and very appealing, but what if I told you that thirty, sixty, and hundredfold has absolutely nothing to do with any of that and has everything to do with empowering the opportunity for you and more so for others?

How many times have you been sitting in a church or watching a religious event or organization and heard them mentioning thirty, sixty, and hundredfold return or some other non-biblical foolishness to encourage you to pay tithes and/or to give financially to one thing or another?

We just went through the definition of faith and how it is derived by hearing. How many of you reading right now put your faith into the thirty, sixty, hundredfold financial return message after you heard someone you thought God had placed in your life preaching or teaching it?

Respectfully, I mean no harm or ill will towards anyone, but truth is truth, and ignorance is ignorance, and I too fell for this hustle. What I realized is that many of those who preach and teach it actually believe it and put their faith in it themselves. It was taught to them, and they are copying what they have been conditioned to do.

I know it's probably hard to believe that you can be enslaved with religion, doctrine, and traditions of men, but this is the whole purpose and agenda of The Way Side, Stony Ground, and Thorns, which is simply to blind you from the truth of the Good Ground and the Great Harvest.

Who you really are is more than likely very far from who you think you are or want to be.

Most of the time, you may not necessarily want to do what you are gifted at doing, although it is mostly effortless for you to do it — so effortless you may completely overlook it and consider it unimportant. Those things that come easily and are common sense for you may not be for others. In the World's System, they may be very useful for business, or to solve problems, or to give advantage in position or rank, or to lead you to a speedy promotion, or to elevate you and put you before great people. You could have an extraordinary talent or skillset that sets you apart as the expert in a particular field or gets the attention of others who resonate with you and want to follow you, request your advice, or hold you in high regard.

This is not by accident or default or coincidental. It's your God Given Purpose, which you must gift to God's people to be a reflection and representation of *The Kingdom of God* and empower God's will on earth as it is in heaven. It is this God-given gift that truly produces the thirty, sixty, hundredfold that you keep hearing all these so-called followers of the Bible preach and teach in complete error.

How frustrating it must be for so many, who are still sitting around waiting on God to show up with this materialized thirty, sixty, hundredfold that does not exist and is never coming in the way they have been conditioned and brainwashed to believe.

- Woe unto those unlearned and ignorant who position themselves to preach and teach and lead God's people without due diligence and hearing from God for themselves.
- Woe unto those who purposely and knowingly mislead, misguide, misinterpret, and falsely proclaim these errors to God's people as truth for their own personal gain and benefit.
- Woe unto those who proclaim the Word of God and utilize biblical principles to manipulate and confuse God's people into placing their faith in a lie.
- Woe unto those who have a platform available to preach, teach, and heal God's people and to provide this Gospel of the Kingdom to all the world for a witness to all nations, yet choose instead to utilize their platform for everything else but the one and only message Jesus preached, which is the *Kingdom*.
- Woe unto those who have turned the House of Prayer into a den of thieves.

This is exactly why your seeds falling on the Good Ground is so important for you and your family.

You must break away from the religion, rules, regulations, denominations, and traditions of men and start seeking the face of God, looking to the hills, asking to receive, seeking to find, and knocking that the door be opened for yourself.

Once you know who you really are, what you really are, and whose you really are and have a truthful and biblical understanding of who Jesus is and why Jesus had to come in the first place, you will begin to understand the original intent and what you originally lost, and that through Jesus, you are in a position to get your power, authority, and dominion, which Adam and Eve gave away in the garden, back from the Devil.

You have consistently and continually been robbed of your love, joy, and peace by the very people who proclaim they know the Bible and have the answers you need to solve all your problems.

Those of you who sincerely seek truth with the right motives and intentions and a pure heart will undoubtedly find it.

Make It Personal: Deuteronomy 31:6

Be strong and of a good courage, fear not, nor be afraid of them: for the LORD your God, the (LORD your God) that does go with (Your Name), the (LORD your God) will not fail (Your Name), nor forsake (Your Name).

In your times of loneliness, when you feel the most discouraged, when life feels heavy, and the pressure of life is upon you, be strengthened and empowered knowing the Creator of Heaven and Earth has you protected and covered.

Make It Personal: Philippians 4:13

(Your Name) can do all things through [Jesus] Christ which strengthens (Your Name).

Make It Personal: 1 John 4:4

You are of God, (Your Name), and have overcome [the spirit of antichrist]: because greater is God that is in (Your Name), than [the spirit of antichrist] that is in the world.

Make It Personal: Romans 8:31

What shall we then say to these things? If God be for (Your Name), who can [successfully] be against (Your Name)?

The seeds falling on the Good Ground make the Great Harvest possible, so make every effort to invest your time and energy in the Good Ground.

Notes:

_____

_____

_____

_____

_____

_____

_____

CHAPTER 4 SUMMARY: MAKE IT PERSONAL

Proverbs 4:7

Wisdom is the principal thing; Therefore _____ needs to get wisdom: And in all _____'s getting [of wisdom], _____ needs to get understanding.

Proverbs 9:10

The fear of the LORD is the beginning of wisdom: and the knowledge of the holy is understanding.

2 Timothy 1:7

For God has not given _____ the spirit of fear, but of power and of love and of a sound mind.

Proverbs 3:5-6

If _____ trusts in the LORD with all _____'s heart; and _____ leans not unto _____'s own understanding and in all _____'s ways _____ acknowledges the LORD, the LORD shall direct _____'s paths.

Proverbs 16:3

If _____ commits _____'s works unto the LORD, then _____'s thoughts shall be established.

John 4:24

God is a Spirit: and _____ must worship God in spirit and in truth.

Genesis 1:26

And God said, Let us make _____ in our image, after our likeness.

John 14:6

Jesus saith unto _____, Jesus is the way, the truth, and the life: _____ cannot come unto the Father [God], but by Jesus.

Romans 8:26-27

Likewise the Spirit also helps _____'s infirmities: for _____ knows not what _____ should pray for as _____ ought: but the Spirit itself makes intercession for _____ with groanings which cannot be uttered. And [God the Father] that searches the hearts knows what is the mind of the [Holy] Spirit, because the [Holy] Spirit makes intercession for _____ according to the will of God.

Genesis 1:27

So God created _____ in his own image, in the image of God created he _____; male and [/or] female created he _____.

Genesis 2:7

And the LORD God formed _____ of the dust of the ground, and breathed into _____'s nostrils the breath of life; and _____ became a living soul.

Jeremiah 1:5

Before God formed _____ in the belly God knew _____; and before _____ came forth out of the womb God sanctified _____ and God ordained _____ to be a [_____] unto the nations.

Isaiah 55:8-9

For God's thoughts are not _____'s thoughts, neither are _____'s ways God's ways, saith the LORD. For as the heavens are higher than the earth, so are God's ways higher than _____'s ways, and God's thoughts [higher] than _____'s thoughts.

Genesis 1:26,28

And God said, let _____ have dominion over the fish of the sea, and over the fowl of the air, and over the cattle, and over all the earth, and over every creeping thing that creeps upon the earth. And God blessed _____, and God said unto _____, Be fruitful, and multiply, and replenish the earth, and subdue it: and have dominion over the fish of the sea, and over the fowl of the air, and over every living thing that moves upon the earth.

2 Timothy 2:15

Study to show yourself approved unto God, a workman that needs not to be ashamed, rightly dividing the word of truth.

John 14:26

But the Comforter, which is the Holy Ghost, whom the Father will send in Jesus' name, the Holy Ghost shall teach _____ ALL Things, and bring ALL Things to _____'s remembrance, whatsoever Jesus has said unto _____.

1 John 2:27

But the anointing which _____ has received of God [in, by, and through Jesus] abides in _____, and _____ need not that any man teach _____: but as the same anointing teach _____ of all things, and is truth, and is no lie, and even as it has taught _____, _____ shall abide in God [in, by, and through Jesus].

1 John 4:4

You are of God, _____, and have overcome [the enemy and the opposition]: because greater is God that is within _____, than [the enemy and opposition] that is in the world.

Philippians 4:13

_____ can do ALL Things through Christ which strengthens _____.

Psalm 23:1

The LORD is _____'s shepherd: _____ shall not want [need or lack].

Romans 12:2

And be not conformed to this world: but be you transformed by the renewing of your mind, that you may prove what is that good, and acceptable, and perfect, will of God.

John 17:14

Jesus has given _____ God's Word; and the world [and the system of the world] has hated _____, because _____ is not of the world [and the system of the world], even as Jesus is not of the world [and the system of the world].

Hosea 4:6

_____ [is] destroyed for lack of knowledge.

Genesis 2:16-17

And the LORD God commanded Adam, saying, Of every tree of the garden you may freely eat: But of the tree of the knowledge of good and evil, you shalt not eat of it: for in the day that you eat thereof you shalt surely die.

Genesis 2:2-3

And Eve said unto the serpent, We may eat of the fruit of the trees of the garden: But of the fruit of the tree which is in the midst of the garden, God has said, You shall not eat of it, neither shall you touch it, lest you die.

Genesis 2:4-5

And the serpent said unto Eve, You shall not surely die: For God does know that in the day you eat thereof, then your eyes shall be opened, and you shall be as gods, knowing good and evil.

Genesis 2:6

And when Eve saw that the tree was good for food, and that it was pleasant to the eyes, and a tree to be desired to make one wise, she took of the fruit thereof, and did eat, and gave also unto Adam with Eve; and Adam did eat.

Hebrews 11:1

Now faith is the substance of things hoped for, the evidence of things not seen.

Romans 10:17

So then faith comes by hearing, and hearing by the word of God.

Deuteronomy 31:6

Be strong and of a good courage, fear not, nor be afraid of them: for the LORD your God, the LORD your God that does go with _____; the LORD your God will not fail _____, nor forsake _____.

1 John 4:4

You are of God, _____, and have overcome [the spirit of antichrist]: because Greater is God that is in _____, than [the spirit of antichrist] that is in the world.

Romans 8:31

What shall we then say to these things? If God be for _____, who can [successfully] be against _____?

Notes:

_____

_____

_____

_____

_____

_____

_____

_____

_____

Good Ground:
Matthew 13:1-9, 18-30, 36-43
Chapter 5: "Great Harvest"

Parable:

The kingdom of heaven is likened unto a man which sowed good seed in his field: But while men slept his enemy came and sowed tares among the wheat, and went his way. But when the blade was sprung up, and brought forth fruit, then appeared tares also. So the servants of the house-holder came and said unto him, Sir, didst not you sow good seed in your field? From whence then has it tares? He said unto them, A enemy has done this. The servants said unto him, Wilt you then that we go and gather them up? But he said, No: lest while you gather up the tares, you root up also the wheat with them. Let both grow together until the harvest: and in the time of harvest I will say to the reapers, Gather you together first the tares, and bind them in bundles to burn them: but gather the wheat to my barn.

Revelation:

He that sows the good seed is the Son of man [Jesus]; The field is the world; the good seed are the children of the kingdom; but the tares are the children of the wicked one; The enemy that sowed them is the Devil; the harvest is the end of the world; and reapers are the angels. As therefore the tares are gathered and burned in the fire: so shall it be in the end of this world. The Son of man [Jesus] shall send forth his angels, and they shall gather out of his kingdom all things that offend, and them which do iniquity; And shall cast them into a furnace of fire: there shall be wailing and gnashing of teeth. Then shall the righteous shine forth as the sun in the kingdom of their Father. Who has ears to hear, let him hear.

The most important aspect of the seed, outside of the ground where it is placed, is what the seed will produce. This is extremely important information that you must fully understand to maximize every day that God allows you to be here on this earth.

Good Seed is sown in Good Ground to obtain a Great Harvest!

As you can clearly read for yourself, this seed, this ground, and this harvest have absolutely nothing to do with money and/or any of the other foolishness I am sure you have heard or will eventually hear.

Unfortunately, this is only one of many purposeful misinterpretations that keep us blinded from the truth and enslaved to religion, denominations, rules and regulations, doctrine, and traditions of men.

The Bible clearly states:

- The world (the field) consists of The Way Side, Stony Ground, Thorns, and Good Ground.
- The world (the field) is where both the Good Seed and the tares are sown.
- Jesus, the Son of man, is the one who sows the Good Seed.
- The Devil, the wicked one, who is the enemy, sows the tares to destroy the Good Seed.
- The Good Seed is the children of the Kingdom, sowed by Jesus, the Son of man.
- The tares are the children of the wicked one, sowed by the Devil.

Simply put, _You Are The Seed!!!_

It is imperative that you read and study your Bible for yourself, so you are not an easy target and do not become one of the many seeds that end up on The Way Side, Stony Ground, or Thorns.

Your goal as the seed is to be placed on Good Ground:

- Hear the Word.
- Understand the Word.
- Bear fruit.
- Bring forth thirty, sixty, hundredfold.

Simply put, thirty, sixty, hundredfold are people being saved, reborn, and renewed to transition from the World's System back to the *Kingdom!*

You owe it to yourself to forget everything you have learned and been taught and begin to seek God and the truth for yourself.

Due diligence is an absolute must, without exceptions, when it comes to knowing God for yourself and building a relationship with Him to be all that you have been ordained and sanctified to be.

Personally, it took me several years of seeking God's face, reading and studying, and the desire to have a one-on-one relationship with God for myself before I realized that I had been brainwashed and conditioned in religion and the traditions of men.

After investing two years of time and study into the Book of Proverbs and then rereading the Bible with eyes to see and ears to hear, I realized that many preach and teach the Bible in error, which ultimately causes confusion.

1 Corinthians 14:33

For God is not the author of confusion, but of peace, as in all churches of the saints.

In addition, most theology, seminary, and other forms of biblical study do not include the one and only message that Jesus preached, which is the *Kingdom!*

Matthew 24:14

And *this gospel of the kingdom* shall be preached in all the world for a witness unto all nations; and then shall the end come.

How many times have you heard this message of the Kingdom being preached to all the nations as instructed by Jesus himself?

It amazes me how the church will preach and teach Jesus and what Jesus did for others, purchase the bumper stickers and T-shirts asking what Jesus would do, but refuse to preach and teach the very message that Jesus preached and instructed us to preach.

This is why I keep highlighting the Kingdom repeatedly. Hold on tight as we dig deeper into the Good Ground, so you can produce a Great Harvest.

I don't want to be repetitive, but it is important that you see it clearly for yourself before we move forward.

Matthew 3:1-2

In those days came John the Baptist, preaching in the wilderness of Judaea, And saying, Repent you, for the *kingdom of heaven* is at hand.

Matthew 4:17

From that time Jesus began to preach, and to say, Repent: for the *kingdom of heaven* is at hand.

Matthew 4:23

And Jesus went about all Galilee, teaching in their synagogues, and *preaching the gospel of the kingdom*, and healing all manner of sickness and all manner of disease among the people.

Matthew 6:10

Thy *kingdom* come. Thy will be done in earth, as it is in heaven.

Matthew 6:33

But seek you first the *kingdom of God*, and God's righteousness; and all these things shall be added unto you.

Matthew 9:35

And Jesus went about all the cities and villages, teaching in their synagogues and *preaching the gospel of the kingdom*, and healing every sickness and every disease among the people.

Matthew 10:7

And as you go, preach, saying, The *kingdom of heaven* is at hand.

Matthew 12:28

But if [Jesus] cast out devils by the Spirit of God, then the *kingdom of God* is come unto you.

These are just a few of the examples of the importance of the kingdom in just the first half of the Book of Matthew, but we are landing on a verse that is extremely important, one that you must understand to overcome the attempts of the enemy.

We have previously discussed The Way Side in Chapter 1 and throughout the book, and I want you to be confident in knowing that this is absolutely the worst ground the seeds (you) can be in, as it is the most detrimental.

Many of you, even while reading this book, have had thoughts of doubt or opposition. Most of you think it is just your own thoughts and feelings, not knowing that the Devil himself has been in your mind, attempting to snatch this information away from you.

There is one subject that makes the Devil himself show up, and that is the *Kingdom!*

It is not mention of religion, rules, regulations, denominations, traditions, faith, the blood, the cross, or even salvation that makes the Devil show up to steal the information away from you. If you do not know or understand the *Kingdom*, then he is still winning and governing your life. You are still mentally under the World's System, whether you are saved or not, if you never take your place and position where you belong.

Parable: Matthew 13:3-4

And Jesus spake many things unto them in parables, saying, Behold, a sower went forth to sow; And when he sowed, some seeds fell by the way side, and the fowls came and devoured them up.

Revelation: Matthew 13:18-19

Hear you therefore the parable of the sower.

When anyone hears the *word of the kingdom*, and understands it not, then comes the wicked one, and catches away that which was sown in his heart. This is he which receives seed by the way side.

How important this message of the *Kingdom* must be.

The Devil's agenda is to make sure you don't understand the Kingdom, so that it is not beneficial or productive for you, and you and your family continue to live the same life under the same system, whether you are saved or not.

Respectfully, we have a whole lot of Way Side Christians, church members, theologians, preachers, teachers, biblical scholars, and the like running around preaching and teaching everything but the Kingdom of Heaven and the Kingdom of God.

Should we even be surprised that there is no authority, dominion, power, and unity if there is no true understanding of the Kingdom?

Once again, it is imperative that we know who we are!

How can we obtain the thirty, sixty, hundredfold if we don't even know that we are the seeds that bring forth the Great Harvest?

The Good Seeds are the children of the Kingdom, but many who are saved don't know their position or recognize the power they truly possess. The Devil is winning in your life if you are out of your God-given position.

Extremely important: if you have not confessed with your mouth and believed in your heart that Jesus is Lord, then you are lost, and you are not saved.

John 3:16-18

For God so loved the world, that he gave his only begotten Son [Jesus], that whosoever believes in [Jesus] shall not perish, but have everlasting life. For God sent not his Son [Jesus] into the world to condemn the world; but that the world through [Jesus] might be saved. [The person] that believes on [Jesus] is not condemned: but [the person] that believes not is condemned already, because [the person] has not believed in the name of the only begotten Son of God [Jesus].

Romans 10:9-13

That if you shalt confess with your mouth the Lord Jesus, and shalt believe in your heart that God raised [Jesus] from the dead, you shalt be saved. For with the heart [the person] believes unto righteousness; and with the mouth confession is made unto salvation. For the scripture saith, Whosoever believes on [Jesus] shall not be ashamed. For there is no difference between the Jew and the Greek: for the same Lord over all is rich unto all that call upon [the Lord]. For whosoever shall call upon the name of the Lord shall be saved.

However, if you have confessed and believed but have not transitioned to the Kingdom mentality and mindset, then you are saved to go to Heaven but still lost right here and right now, which is the most important part of your purpose here on Earth.

We must all understand that a person cannot be lost unless they were initially, once upon a time, already where they were supposed to be. This is yet another reason why you must know who you are, so you can make every effort to find your way back to where you belong.

There is no way to accurately and successfully do what God has directed us to do if we do not understand the Kingdom of God and the Kingdom of Heaven.

People must stop trying to live out a Kingdom lifestyle inside the World's System!

There must be a transition, a renewing of the mind, a rebirth, and a restoration from the World's System.

The Devil knows the Bible and makes every attempt to keep you from knowing who you really are. This is how he can maintain control and power over you and keep you in the shackles and chains of the World's System, enslaved by religion, rules, regulations, and traditions of men.

The Devil's goal is to eliminate the Good Ground and the Great Harvest for you personally and to prolong the inevitable as much as he possibly can. The less Bible we know and understand, the more the Devil can do to us and continue to get away with it.

Why do you think there are so many religions, denominations, options, and choices available to you?

How is it that there are thousands of ways to God available to you when the Bible clearly tells us that there is only one way?

When you eliminate unity, you empower division, and to divide is to conquer and overcome.

Matthew 12:25

And Jesus knew their thoughts, and said unto them, Every kingdom divided against itself is brought to desolation: and every city or house divided against itself shall not stand: And if Satan cast out Satan, he is divided against himself: how shall then his kingdom stand?

The Devil is crafty, and within every lie there is truth. The Devil utilizes this same biblical principle right now today throughout the world to cause division and confusion, to eliminate the Good Ground and the Great Harvest.

Preacher against preacher, denomination against denomination, religion against religion, government against government, human against human, culture against culture, family against family, and ultimately wrong against wrong all brings nothing more than *Division!*

How will the message of the Kingdom reach all nations if everyone is divided and there is no unity?

God placed you in the field as the Good Seed with a purpose to find Good Ground to fulfill Kingdom Purpose with a Great Harvest of thirty, sixty, hundredfold.

Matthew 9:37-38

Then saith [Jesus] unto his disciples, The harvest truly is plenteous, but the labourers are few; Pray you therefore the Lord of the harvest, that he will send forth labourers into his harvest.

The children of the Kingdom are the laborers. We need more Good Seeds on Good Ground.

During one of my interactions with God through Bible study and prayer, I was asked, "How long will you be a beautiful tree with no fruit?"

I then internally asked myself, "How long will I be a beautiful tree with strong roots and nice bark, with great branches and bright green leaves but no fruit?"

John 15:1-2

[Jesus] is the true vine, and [God the] Father is the husbandman. Every branch in [Jesus] that bears no fruit [God the Father] takes away: and every branch that bears fruit, [God the Father] purges it, that it may bring forth more fruit.

Make It Personal: John 15:4-5

Abide in [Jesus], and [Jesus] in (Your Name). As the branch cannot bear fruit of itself, except it abide in the vine; no more can (Your Name), except (Your Name) abide in [Jesus]. [Jesus] is the vine, (Your Name) [is] the branches: [if] (Your Name) abides in [Jesus], and [Jesus] in (Your Name), the same brings forth much fruit: for without [Jesus] (Your Name) can do nothing.

We can't just look, think, and feel the part; we must actively be and do to empower the Kingdom of God within and be a light that shines for others to see Truth over the lie. The bearing of much fruit is the truth and power of thirty, sixty, hundredfold, and this is the Great Harvest.

Simply put, being saved for self and going on living our own lives is biblically not enough, and not understanding the importance of the Kingdom is detrimental to the Great Harvest.

Matthew 21:43

Therefore says [Jesus] unto you, The kingdom of God shall be taken from you, and given to a nation bringing forth the fruits thereof.

The Great Harvest is bringing forth the fruits of the Kingdom of God.

How did religion, churches, preachers and teachers get so off track when it is right in the Bible, staring us all in the face, plain as day?

Maybe if we would stop turning the house of prayer into an entertainment factory to appease to the natural man instead of the spiritual man, things would be better.

The church seems to be filled with ungodly non-biblical distractions, whether it be treating it like a movie theater or a concert with the lights off, high-fiving and speaking pointless quotes we don't even believe to our neighbors, twirling flags, singing depressing slavery songs, doing fake and phony "Holy Spirit" dances, begging and pleading for money under false pretenses, or other demonic and satanic activities that I won't elaborate on in this book.

Is it just me, or do most churches and religious organizations seem to spend way more time talking about tithes and offerings and collecting your money than they do talking about salvation?

Now ask yourself the same question in relation to what you have heard about the Kingdom.

How can we really be surprised? Respectfully, the largest denomination in the world doesn't even pray to God when they are praying, still tells their sins to a man, thinks sprinkles of water will save them, reads out of a pamphlet instead of the Bible, violates and traumatizes our children, and does way more demonic and satanic things that I won't get into in this book.

For those of you who read the Bible, ask yourself who Jesus is usually talking to when He seems annoyed or aggravated.

The only time Jesus comes out of character (so to speak) or changes His behavior is when He speaks against religious people attacking the Good Ground and the Great Harvest with rules, regulations, and traditions of men that contradict the Kingdom of God.

Warning: Matthew 16:6-7

Then Jesus said unto them, Take heed and beware of the leaven of the Pharisees and of the Sadducees.

And they reasoned among themselves, saying, It is because we have taken no bread.

Revelation: Matthew 16:11-12

How is it that you do not understand that I spake it not to you concerning bread, that you should beware of the leaven of the Pharisees and of the Sadducees?

Then understood they how that he bade them not beware of leaven of bread, *but of the doctrine* of the Pharisees and of the Sadducees.

Remember, the Devil has no new tricks and is the originator of nothing. The warning Jesus gives to his disciples in the Bible is the same exact warning Jesus gives us right now today.

Take heed and *beware of doctrines* that promote religion and the traditions of men, that enslave you with rules and regulations to bind you in the very system that Jesus came to get you out of.

Think about it: who was Jesus' enemy in the Bible? Who did He argue with? Who were the ones who were envious, jealous, and hateful towards Him and ultimately plotted to have him killed? Now ask yourself: why?

John 11:47-48

Then gathered the chief priests and the Pharisees a council, and said, What do we? For [Jesus] does many miracles. If we leave [Jesus] alone, all [people] will believe on [Jesus]: and the Romans shall come and take away both our place and nation.

The Elders, Priests, Scribes, Pharisees, Sadducees, and those of the Temple (which today would be the church) are the ones who did not accept Jesus. Sadly, with all the religions and denominations, this is exactly what challenges us today.

Where is the Good Ground and the Great Harvest in the church?

The Kingdom of God and Kingdom of Heaven is not being preached, and it is the *only* message that Jesus preached.

To address another huge misconception and misinterpretation among so many, The Kingdom of Heaven and the Kingdom of God are *not* the same thing in the natural sense, in terms of location, although spiritually the terms are used interchangeably.

Jesus is the *King*, the Kingdom of Heaven is where the King resides, and the Kingdom of God, sometimes referred to as the Kingdom of Heaven, is the representation and reflection of the Kingdom here on Earth.

This takes wisdom, knowledge, and understanding to fully comprehend. Do not allow those who do not fully grasp the Kingdom of God to confuse you into thinking that every time you read or hear the term it refers to Heaven or going to Heaven, because that is biblically inaccurate.

Luke 17:20-21

And when [Jesus] was demanded of the Pharisees, when the kingdom of God should come, [Jesus] answered them and said, The kingdom of God comes not with observation: Neither shall they say, Lo here! Or, lo there! For, behold, <u>*The Kingdom of God is Within You.*</u>

How simplistic is that verse?

How is the Kingdom of God in Heaven if Jesus just clearly and plainly stated that the Kingdom of God does not come with observation, it's not here, it's not there, but it is within you?

If it is still difficult, then simply ask yourself where you are. Are you in Heaven? No! Then the Kingdom of God is not in Heaven, but it is within you here in Earth as it is in Heaven.

Matthew 6:9-10

After this manner therefore pray you: Our Father which art in Heaven, [Holy] be your name. Your kingdom come. Your will be done in Earth, as it is in Heaven.

The will of God being done in the Earth as it is in Heaven is the representation and the reflection of the Kingdom of Heaven in the Earth, which is the Kingdom of God within you.

Make It Personal: 2 Corinthians 5:20

Now then (Your Name) is an ambassador for [Jesus] Christ....

Kingdom Ambassador:

An Official Representative sent by God to the World's System to promote and exemplify the Kingdom and the culture of the Kingdom in Word and Action, to teach a Kingdom Mentality and a Kingdom Mindset to fulfill Kingdom Purpose.

As you can see, it is extremely important that you understand your assignment, so that the Good Ground brings forth a Great Harvest.

You are not here for nothing. Every day you wake up, you have purpose to fulfill. If you are still here, then you are still on your God-given assignment to obtain thirty, sixty, hundredfold!

Everything you are searching for to fulfill purpose and to fill the voids in your life can be found in God and the Kingdom of God. This is the Good Ground and the Great Harvest.

I thank God for revelation and confirmation.

I write this book in obedience to the instruction and direction given to me by God, to allow the Spirit of God to use me as a vessel to impart wisdom, knowledge, and understanding of biblical truth of the Kingdom of God.

I write with a heavy heart, knowing most will not accept the Truth because it does not fit their conditioned and brainwashed views, which are based on the religion and traditions of men.

John 8:31-32

Then said Jesus to those Jews who believed on [Jesus], If you continue in [Jesus'] word, then are you [Jesus'] disciples indeed; And you shall know the truth, and the truth shall make you free.

Until one knows who they really are and their original purpose, they are enslaved to the lies being taught. When one does not know, believe, or admit that they can be enslaved, then they cannot be made free.

I know who I am, and I know the assignment that God has given me. Just like every Prophet and Disciple of the Bible, I am prepared to not be accepted, appreciated, or respected and to be judged, mistreated, and overlooked because I don't fit the worldly mold.

Matthew 10:22, 24, 32-33, 36, 38

And you shall be hated of all [people] for [Jesus'] name's sake: but [the person] that endures to the end shall be saved. The disciple is not above his master, nor the servant above his lord. Whosoever therefore shall confess [Jesus] before [people], that person will [Jesus] confess also before [God the] Father which is in heaven. But whosoever shall deny [Jesus] before [people], that person will [Jesus] also deny before [God the] Father which is in heaven. And a [person's] foes shall be [people] of [that person's] own household. And [a person] that takes not their cross, and follows after [Jesus], is not worthy of [Jesus].

I pray that, even in my absence, this book will continue to empower the truth of the Kingdom of God in others and add fruit to my branches. I pray that you will begin or continue to add more and more fruit to your own branches and ultimately the Great Harvest.

CHAPTER 5 SUMMARY: MAKE IT PERSONAL

1 Corinthians 14:33

For God is not the author of confusion, but of peace, as in all churches of the saints.

Matthew 24:14

And *this gospel of the kingdom* shall be preached in all the world for a witness unto all nations; and then shall the end come.

Matthew 3:1-2

In those days came John the Baptist, preaching in the wilderness of Judaea, And saying, Repent you, for the *kingdom of heaven* is at hand.

Matthew 4:17

From that time Jesus began to preach, and to say, Repent: for the *kingdom of heaven* is at hand.

Matthew 4:23

And Jesus went about all Galilee, teaching in their synagogues, and *preaching the gospel of the kingdom*, and healing all manner of sickness and all manner of disease among the people.

Matthew 6:10

Thy *kingdom* come. Thy will be done in earth, as it is in heaven.

Matthew 6:33

But seek _____ first the *kingdom of God*, and God's righteousness; and all these things shall be added unto _____.

Matthew 9:35

And Jesus went about all the cities and villages, teaching in their synagogues and *preaching the gospel of the kingdom*, and healing every sickness and every disease among the people.

Matthew 10:7

And as _____ go, preach, saying, The *kingdom of heaven* is at hand.

Matthew 12:28

But if [Jesus] cast out devils by the Spirit of God, then the *kingdom of God* is come unto you.

Matthew 13:3-4

And Jesus spake many things unto them in parables, saying, Behold, a sower went forth to sow; And when he sowed, some seeds fell by the way side, and the fowls came and devoured them up.

Matthew 13:18-19

Hear you therefore the parable of the sower.

When _____ hears the *word of the kingdom*, and understands it not, then comes the wicked one, and catches away that which was sown in _____'s heart. This is _____ which receives seed by the way side.

John 3:16-18

For God so loved _____, that he gave his only begotten Son [Jesus], that [if] _____ believes in [Jesus] _____ shall not perish, but have everlasting life. For God sent not his Son [Jesus] into the world to condemn _____; but that _____ through [Jesus] might be saved. [If] _____ believes on [Jesus] _____ is not condemned: but [if] _____ believes not _____ is condemned already, because _____ has not believed in the name of the only begotten Son of God [Jesus].

Romans 10:9-13

That if _____ shalt confess with _____'s mouth the Lord Jesus, and shalt believe in _____'s heart that God raised [Jesus] from the dead, _____ shalt be saved. For with the heart _____ believes unto righteousness; and with the mouth confession is made unto salvation. For the scripture saith, [if] _____ believes on [Jesus] _____ shall not be ashamed. For there is no difference between the Jew and the Greek: for the same Lord over all is rich unto all that call upon [the Lord]. For [if] _____ shall call upon the name of the Lord _____ shall be saved.

Matthew 12:25

And Jesus knew their thoughts, and said unto them, Every kingdom divided against itself is brought to desolation: and every city or house divided against itself shall not stand: And if Satan cast out Satan, he is divided against himself: how shall then his kingdom stand?

Matthew 9:37-38

Then saith [Jesus] unto _____, The harvest truly is plenteous, but the labourers are few; Pray you therefore the Lord of the harvest, that he will send forth _____ into his harvest.

John 15:1-2

[Jesus] is the true vine, and [God the] Father is the husbandman. Every branch in [Jesus] that bears no fruit [God the Father] takes away: and every branch that bears fruit, [God the Father] purges it, that it may bring forth more fruit.

John 15:4-5

Abide in [Jesus], and [Jesus] in _____. As the branch cannot bear fruit of itself, except it abide in the vine; no more can _____, except _____ abide in [Jesus]. [Jesus] is the vine, _____ are the branches: [if] _____ abides in [Jesus], and [Jesus] in _____, the same brings forth much fruit: for without [Jesus] _____ can do nothing.

Matthew 21:43

Therefore says [Jesus] unto you, The kingdom of God shall be taken from you, and given to a nation bringing forth the fruits thereof.

Matthew 16:6-7

Then Jesus said unto _____, Take heed and beware of the leaven of the Pharisees and of the Sadducees. And they reasoned among themselves, saying, It is because we have taken no bread.

Matthew 16:11-12

How is it that you do not understand that I spake it not to you concerning bread, that you should beware of the leaven of the Pharisees and of the Sadducees?

Then understood _____ how that he bade them not beware of leaven of bread, *but of the doctrine* of the Pharisees and of the Sadducees.

John 11:47-48

Then gathered the chief priests and the Pharisees a council, and said, What do we? For [Jesus] does many miracles. If we leave [Jesus] alone, all [people] will believe on [Jesus]: and the Romans shall come and take away both our place and nation.

Luke 17:20-21

And when [Jesus] was demanded of the Pharisees, when the kingdom of God should come, [Jesus] answered them and said, The kingdom of God comes not with observation: Neither shall they say, Lo here! Or, lo there! For, behold, *The Kingdom of God is Within You.*

Matthew 6:9-10

After this manner therefore pray you: Our Father which art in Heaven, [Holy] be your name. Your kingdom come. Your will be done in Earth, as it is in Heaven.

2 Corinthians 5:20

Now then _____ is an ambassador for [Jesus] Christ....

John 8:31-32

Then said Jesus to _____ who believed on [Jesus], If _____ continue in [Jesus'] word, then _____ is [Jesus'] disciple indeed; And _____ shall know the truth, and the truth shall make _____ free.

Matthew 10:22, 24, 32-33, 36, 38

And _____ shall be hated of all [people] for [Jesus'] name's sake: but [if] _____ endures to the end _____ shall be saved. _____ is not above his master, nor _____ above his lord. [If] _____ therefore shall confess [Jesus] before [people], _____ will [Jesus] confess also before [God the] Father which is in heaven. But [if] _____ shall deny [Jesus] before [people], _____ will [Jesus] also deny before [God the] Father which is in heaven. And _____'s foes shall be [people] of _____'s own household. And [if] _____ takes not _____'s cross, and follows after [Jesus], _____ is not worthy of [Jesus].

The world consists of:

- The Way Side
- Stony Ground
- Thorns
- Good Ground

The world is where:

- The Good Seed is sown.
- The tares are sown.

Good Seed:

- Jesus, the Son of man, sows the Good Seed.
- The Good Seed is the children of the Kingdom.

The Tares:

- The Devil, the wicked one, sows the tares.
- The tares are the children of the wicked one.

Revelation:

- You are the Seed that determines the Harvest.
- Good Seed has the Kingdom of God within.
- Tares have the Devil within.

Notes:

Appendix

As I write this, I find myself shaking my head and holding back tears because I know the consequences of awakening minds to Truth. However, I also know the consequences of not telling the Truth when it has been placed in you to fulfill *Kingdom Purpose*.

Make It Personal: Matthew 10:27-28

What Jesus tells _____ in darkness, that speak _____ in the light: and what _____ hears in the ear, that preach _____ upon the housetops. And fear not them which kill the body, but are not able to kill the soul: but rather fear God which is able to destroy both soul and body in hell.

Make It Personal: Matthew 16:24-26

Then said Jesus unto _____, If _____ will come after Jesus, let _____ deny [self], and take up _____'s cross, and follow Jesus. For whosoever will save their life shall lose it: and whosoever will lose their life for Jesus's sake shall find it. For what is _____ to profit if _____ shall gain the whole world, and lose _____'s own soul? Or what shall _____ give in exchange for _____'s soul?

If God allows me to reach just one of you who actually gets it and begins to think differently by the renewing of your mind, and God opens your eyes to see and opens your ears to hear, then whatever challenges, trials, and tribulations that come my way will have not been in vain and will be more than worth it to me.

Unfortunately, it took me 37 years to figure out that everything that I have and everything that God has enabled me to do is for someone else. You will not understand the full concept of the Good Ground and the Great Harvest until you have accepted this truth for yourself. The very gift that God has blessed you with is not for selfishness or greed but to share with others, to empower them to transition their minds to *Kingdom Purpose.*

Eliminate the Way Side, Stony Ground, and Thorns, find the Good Ground, and produce a Great Harvest!

We must all get to the place where we make a conscious decision to live our lives with purpose rather than just existing, going through the purposeful traps, and waiting to die.

For one to have only lived to die is for one to have never lived at all!

Learn to start living on purpose, with purpose, and make it *Kingdom Purpose.*

Bonus Chapter: Beware of the Leaven

Warning: Matthew 16:6-7

Then Jesus said unto them, Take heed and beware of the leaven of the Pharisees and of the Sadducees.

And they reasoned among themselves, saying, It is because we have taken no bread.

Revelation: Matthew 16:11-12

How is it that you do not understand that I spake it not to you concerning bread, that you should beware of the leaven of the Pharisees and of the Sadducees?

Then understood they how that he bade them not beware of leaven of bread, *but of the doctrine* of the Pharisees and of the Sadducees.

I mentioned this briefly in Chapter 5, but I know this is a crucial part of your growth and development. Please understand, there are people in high places who do not want you to know this information because it disrupts their control over you and your family and threatens their man-made positions.

The more Bible you know and the closer you become with God in building a real relationship, the more you will begin to see that we have been manipulated and lied to all of our lives, both by the World's System and by the church, which is supposed to be our escape from the system but is really nothing more than a transfer from one demonic system of slavery to another.

Pay attention, and you will realize that the goal is to keep you from knowing the Truth, no matter what the situation may be. The less truth you know, the easier a target you are to keep enslaved for whatever the purpose or agenda is in that moment.

The less you know, the worse off you and your family will be! Lack of knowledge destroys!

We have been so programmed and conditioned to just take everything that we are told as truth — so much so that the lie has become truth and the truth is nonexistent in most minds.

We now live in a society where right is wrong and wrong is right. Even the church, as a majority, has taken God, Jesus, the Holy Spirit, the Bible, Prayer, and the Truth out of the equation.

Isaiah 5:20

Woe unto them that call evil good, and good evil; that put darkness for light, and light for darkness; that put bitter for sweet, and sweet for bitter!

They are promoting, advertising, and marketing a Kingdom lifestyle but not giving you the biblical principles to obtain it. This is because most of them have no idea what the Kingdom really is or how to obtain it themselves, and the ones who do don't want you to know because it threatens their position.

Matthew 23:15

Woe unto you, scribes and Pharisees, hypocrites! For you compass sea and land to make one proselyte, and when he is made, you make him twofold more the child of hell than yourselves.

Read very earnestly and try to hear my words as you are reading; this is the exact same thing that is happening to the church as a whole today. They are still preaching and teaching the same messages that Jesus rebuked.

Jesus clearly states that the "church" people are the child of Hell, which means that with all their religion, rules, regulations, and traditions of men, they are not the children of the Kingdom but are instead assisting the Devil as the tares to destroy the wheat.

Remember, it is the Good Ground that brings forth good fruit and the Great Harvest, but most reside in The Way Side, Stony Ground, and Thorns. This will never produce the thirty, sixty, hundredfold of good fruit.

Matthew 7:15-20

Beware of false prophets which come to you in sheep's clothing, but inwardly they are ravening wolves. You shall know them by their fruits. Do men gather grapes of thorns, or figs of thistles? Even so every good tree brings forth good fruit; but a corrupt tree brings forth evil fruit. A good tree cannot bring forth evil fruit, neither can a corrupt tree bring forth good fruit. Every tree that brings not forth good fruit is hewn down and cast into the fire. Wherefore by their fruits you shall know them.

Look at the church (little c) today and ask yourself honestly: do you see good fruit, or do you see attempts to retrieve good fruit from a corrupt tree?

Respectfully, this is not me being judgmental or negative. All you have to do is turn on your TV, scroll through your computer, listen to the radio, or have a basic conversation, and you will soon realize that the system is corrupt.

You will know them by the fruit they produce.

Man is always interfering with truth and attempting to be God, just like the Devil, so it is not hard to figure out where these thoughts, ideas, and concepts come from.

You cannot fulfill your purpose until you truly know who you are!

The Devil's goal is to keep you from ever knowing who you are so that you will never be a threat to his agenda.

John 10:10

The thief comes not, but for to steal, and to kill, and to destroy.

The Devil wants to steal, kill, and ultimately destroy your identity so that you remain bound, unlearned, and ignorant of the truth of who you really are and remain incarcerated in the World's System.

Let's not forget who the Bible is written to and who the Bible is talking about, from the Old Testament to the New Testament.

Paul is not writing letters to the world elites, governments, politicians, casinos, clubs, liquor stores, smoke shops, supremacist groups, gang members, or all the other groups and entities religion puts so much focus on. Think about it. Who is Paul writing these letters in the Bible to?

Again, this is nothing new. The Devil has been using the exact same tricks and hustle that he knows works to keep us confused and blinded from the Truth. This includes many standing behind the pulpit.

Jesus instructed us to Beware of the Leaven, which is to beware of the doctrine. This means you can't be naive and gullible and believe everything someone tells you about God or the Bible. You must build a personal relationship with God for yourself.

Proverbs 23:1-3, 6-8

When you sit to eat with a ruler, consider diligently what is before you: And put a knife to your throat, if you be a [person] given to appetite. Be not desirous of [the ruler's] dainties: for they are deceitful meat. Eat you not the bread of [the ruler] that has an evil eye, neither desire you [the ruler's] dainty meats. For as [the ruler] thinks in [the ruler's] heart, so is [the ruler]: Eat and drink, says [the ruler] to you; but [the ruler's] heart is not with you. The morsel which you have eaten, shalt you vomit up, and lose your sweet words.

As a person thinks in their heart [mind], so is that person. The Bible refers to the ruler in a negative sense for this situation, although the statement stands for either a positive or a negative depending on the person and their motives.

Many books have been written, and messages have been preached regarding verse 7 for as long as I can remember. However, in these verses Solomon, like Jesus, also instructs us to be wise and to consider the information that we receive from others, especially when they may not have our best interests in mind.

Most people don't even understand that these verses have nothing to do with food or the ruler but more so the lack of due diligence and accepting information provided that is not beneficial or productive for you.

- Beware of the Leaven.
- Beware of the Doctrine.
- Beware of information provided by those whose hearts are not with you.

Revelation: Proverbs 23:1-3, 6-8

When you sit with a person have the ears to hear with wisdom and due diligence what is being proposed: And put a knife to your throat if you are a person who is willing to accept and listen to any thing someone has to say without doing your due diligence. Be not desirous of deceitful propositions. Do not adhere to the false doctrine and information of a person who has an evil eye, neither should you desire the deceitful proposition. For as a person thinks in their heart so is that person; Take the proposition, the person says to you; but the person's heart does not have the right intentions and motives, and they are not doing things in your best interest. If you decide to accept the deceitful proposition and adhere to the false doctrine and the information provided, you too will begin to speak and repeat the false doctrine and information you accepted and lose your true self in the process.

Faith in the contradiction of God's Word comes by hearing the contradiction of God's Word.

Sadly, many people behind the pulpit do not have your best interests in mind and purposely keep you as far away from the truth as possible for as long as possible with the contradictions of God's Word, for their own selfishness and greed.

The Devil has weaponized man-made religion, traditions of men, and false doctrine to cause fear, hurt, confusion, hate, and ultimately death in the lives of so many people.

I, Brian P. Lucas, am boldly stating, no more! *Wake Up!* Don't be so easily distracted from your purpose!

Become the <u>Men</u> and <u>Women</u> that God has already ordained and sanctified you to be before you entered your mothers' wombs.

Stop living your life just to die one day and then go to Heaven. This is not the gospel and is just another form of religion.

Walk in your authority, dominion, and power to fulfill Kingdom Purpose!

God has planted you here in the Earth to find the Good Ground to produce good fruit for the Great Harvest. Your mission, direction, instruction, and obligation are here on the Earth, not in Heaven.

Read how Abraham, Isaac, Jacob, Elijah, Daniel, Samson, Joseph, Moses, Noah, Joshua, David, Solomon, Isaiah, Jeremiah, Ezekiel, Jonah, John the Baptist, Peter, James, John, Paul, Ruth, Rahab, Abigail, Pharaoh's Daughter, the Samaritan woman at the well, Mary Magdalene, and even Jesus himself played vital roles in fulfilling God's plans.

Excluding Jesus, every one of these men and women had personal challenges and failures to overcome, and God still utilized them and their gifts to fulfill His purpose.

You are nothing less than the greatness you read about in the lives of these men and women and so many more throughout the Bible, who sacrificed self for the Good Ground and the Great Harvest.

BONUS CHAPTER: MAKE IT PERSONAL

Matthew 16:6-7

Then Jesus said unto them, Take heed and beware of the leaven of the Pharisees and of the Sadducees.

And they reasoned among themselves, saying, It is because we have taken no bread.

Matthew 16:11-12

How is it that you do not understand that I spake it not to you concerning bread, that you should beware of the leaven of the Pharisees and of the Sadducees? Then understood they how that he bade them not beware of leaven of bread, *but of the doctrine* of the Pharisees and of the Sadducees.

Isaiah 5:20

Woe unto them that call evil good, and good evil; that put darkness for light, and light for darkness; that put bitter for sweet, and sweet for bitter!

Matthew 23:15

Woe unto you, scribes and Pharisees, hypocrites! For you compass sea and land to make one proselyte, and when he is made, you make him twofold more the child of hell than yourselves.

Matthew 7:15-20

Beware of false prophets which come to _____ in sheep's clothing, but inwardly they are ravening wolves. _____ shall know them by their fruits. Do men gather grapes of thorns, or figs of thistles? Even so every good tree brings forth good fruit; but a corrupt tree brings forth evil fruit. A good tree cannot bring forth evil fruit, neither can a corrupt tree bring forth good fruit. Every tree that brings not forth good fruit is hewn down and cast into the fire. Wherefore by their fruits _____ shall know them.

John 10:10

The thief comes not, but for to steal, and to kill, and to destroy _____.

Proverbs 23:1-3, 6-8

When _____ sit to eat with a ruler, consider diligently what is before _____: And put a knife to _____'s throat, if _____ be a [person] given to appetite. Be not desirous of [the ruler's] dainties: for they are deceitful meat. Eat _____ not the bread of [the ruler] that has an evil eye, neither desire _____ [the ruler's] dainty meats. For as [the ruler] thinks in [the ruler's] heart, so is [the ruler]: Eat and drink, says [the ruler] to _____; but [the ruler's] heart is not with _____. The morsel which _____ have eaten, shalt _____ vomit up, and lose _____'s sweet words.

Revelation: Proverbs 23:1-3, 6-8

When _____ sits with a person _____ [needs to] have the ears to hear with wisdom and due diligence what is being proposed: And put a knife to _____'s throat if _____ is a person who is willing to accept and listen to any thing someone has to say without doing _____'s due diligence.

Be not desirous of deceitful propositions. Do not adhere to the false doctrine and information of a person who has an evil eye, neither should _____ desire the deceitful proposition.

For as a person thinks in their heart so is that person; Take the proposition; the person says to _____; but the person's heart does not have the right intentions and motives, and they are not doing things in _____'s best interest.

If _____ decides to accept the deceitful proposition and adhere to the false doctrine and the information provided, _____ too will begin to speak and repeat the false doctrine and information _____ has accepted and lose _____'s true self in the process.

Beware of the:

- Leaven/Doctrine of man and religion.
- Information provided by those whose hearts are not with you.
- False prophets which come to you in sheep's clothing.

The Devil's goal is to:

- Steal
- Kill
- Destroy
- Keep you from ever knowing who you are.

You must understand:

- We now live in a society where right is wrong and wrong is right.
- Faith in the contradiction of God's Word comes by hearing the contradiction of God's Word.
- The lack of knowledge destroys.

Notes:

The Conclusion

You are a spirit who comes from God and is created by God, placed here on Earth to fulfill *Kingdom Purpose* to be a representation and reflection of the *Kingdom*. You have been ordained and sanctified to use your God-Given Gift to Seek and to Save that which was lost and bring them back home.

As a speaking spirit, you have been given the power, authority, and dominion as a child of the *Living God* to be a joint heir, a citizen, an ambassador, and most importantly a servant to the *King*.

You have been ordained and sanctified with a specific gift that enables you to have a strong positive impact on God's people, to enable the necessary changes in mentality and mindset that will truly free them from the distractions, tricks, and traps of the *Way Side*, *Stony Ground*, and *Thorns*, which only promote fear and the contradiction of God's Word.

Seeds scattered on Good Ground will bring forth a Great Harvest.

My prayer is that, even right now as you are reading this, the Holy Spirit warms your heart and simultaneously chills your body with an unexplainable and undeniable sensation that allows you to know without any doubts that you are not alone and you have safety and protection and a comforter in the name above all names, the name where every knee shall bow and every mouth shall confess that <u>*JESUS THE CHRIST IS LORD.*</u>

Father God in Heaven, Holy is Your Name. Your *Kingdom* come and Your will be done *in Earth* as it is in Heaven. Father God, empower your Word and your Truth to saturate the hearts and minds of those who search and seek to understand their purpose in life. Let this book and the information it contains be a part of the seed that falls onto Good Ground to bring forth a Great Harvest in the lives of those who read it, in this generation and in generations to come. Father God, in Jesus' Name, by way of the Power of the Holy Spirit, I pray that you enable the readers' Eyes to be Open to See, that you will give them Spiritual Ears to Hear, that they will fully understand to Seek Ye First the *Kingdom of God* and Your Righteousness, and that they will Seek and to Save that which was lost so that Seed will fall onto Good Ground and bring forth a Great Harvest. Father God, let your Mercy, Grace, Favor, and Peace, which surpasses all understanding, be upon each reader. Let the Confession of their Mouth and the Belief in their Heart declare that your Son Jesus the Christ is Lord unto Salvation, and let them walk in Your Ordained and Sanctified Will to fulfill God-Given Purpose. All the Honor, Glory, and Praise is Yours, Father God. Thank you for the Holy Spirit. In Jesus' Name I pray, Amen.

About the Author

Most importantly, above anything and everything else, I believe in and I trust the God in Heaven, who is the God of the Bible. I believe in God the Father, Jesus the Christ, and the Holy Spirit. I believe that Jesus is the Son of God and that Jesus died on the cross for my sins, transgressions, and unrighteousness. I believe in the resurrection, that Jesus was raised from the dead and that Jesus now sits on the right hand of God the Father with all power in Heaven and on Earth. I respectfully believe without compromise, doubts, or any second thoughts that Jesus is the one and only way to God the Father and that Jesus is the one and only way to receive Salvation and Forgiveness by the Mercy and Grace of God.

Now, am I an angel, holier than thou, full of righteousness by my own power, religious, or perfect? No!

Frankly, if I were or if anyone else actually could be, then there would be no need for Jesus or a Savior, because we would just press our holiness button and save ourselves.

I am nothing without God; this book and everything else I possess belongs to God, so I refuse to compromise on my faith and belief in God.

I am but a lonely voice in the wilderness that has experienced my own personal road to Damascus and has been awakened to a glimpse of the truth that every human being searches for.

One great thing about truth is that it is always true. Whether it's coming from a doctor or a janitor, a multi-millionaire or someone living in poverty, someone driving a luxury car or someone riding a bicycle, a dope dealer on the corner or a preacher behind the pulpit, the truth is always the truth!

Truth in word will always resonate with those who are seeking it. My birds will know my feathers and flock with me, and the sheep I am responsible for will know my voice. I will resonate with them, and they will resonate with me.

I am that I am, not what the world tells me or attempts to market and advertise me to be.

My life forever changed when I came to the simple conclusion that the world owes me nothing and that I am not entitled to anything outside of my faith that I have not worked for or willed my way.

I now understand the importance of having eyes to see and ears to hear, which enable me to see through the deception the world consistently promotes to the walking blind, who have their eyes wide shut.

I strongly believe that ethics, morals, and character still mean something today, no matter what this new world is shoving down our throats!

I promote unity over division, I support equality over slavery, and I respect hard work and not laziness.

Mentality and mindset are key: stand for something, or you will fall for anything!

About the Author

Here is my bio summed up:

I once was lost, but now I am found; I once was blind, but now I see.

My only goal and purpose in life is to open the eyes of as many people as possible while I am still here, so that each day I am hopefully putting a smile on God's face.

Every day, I want to imagine God saying, "Well done, good and faithful servant."

I am that I am because of who Jesus is.

I have what I have because of what Jesus has.

I can do what I do because of what Jesus did for me on the cross.

I am nothing without Jesus!

Every experience and accomplishment I am blessed to possess and all my joy comes from the aforementioned.

Sincerely and respectfully,

Brian P. Lucas
BRIAN P. LUCAS

Author: Brian P. Lucas

Discover the quickest, easiest, most convenient way to reach your personal goals in life, by living on your own terms and by your own definitions, and ultimately determining your own personal definition of perfection. If you are ready to find out who you really are, and begin to live by your own definitions, and you are truly interested in succeeding and utilizing a system that's proven to work, this may be the book for you.

Author: Brian P. Lucas

Multiple efforts focused on the same goals will reap multiple rewards and truly experience the results of unity. Unity begins with you and the power of unity eliminates lack, pride, and most importantly division. To divide is to conquer and division only destroys and brings destruction to you and your family. Unity is the key and nothing will be withheld from those who possess The True Power of Unity.

Author: Brian P. Lucas

Renew and transition your mentality and mindset back to the original intent and to your *Rightful Position* so you are able to walk in the authority, dominion, and power that you were initially equipped with from the very beginning. The Enemy and the Opposition of your elevation, growth, and development has purposely instilled fear, chaos, and confusion to keep you as far away from the Truth as possible so you remain blind and in darkness.

<u>Back to the Garden</u> shines light in the darkness and provides the only Truth that will make you free from the rules, regulations, religion, and traditions of men. You must empower the *Kingdom of God* which is within you to eliminate the brainwashing and conditioning influences of the World's System.

God has ordained you and sanctified you to be a great representation and reflection of the *Kingdom*. You are fearfully and wonderfully made in the image and likeness of God, and you are special because there is only one you.

You must *Know Who You Are* to fulfill *Kingdom Purpose*.

Author: Brian P. Lucas

Simply Believe highlights John's Walk with Jesus in an easy-to-read format with a purposely repetitive verse-by-verse breakdown.

Brian P. Lucas provides you with a very direct and engaging commentary to empower you to have a greater understanding of The Gospel According to St. John.

It is imperative that you read the Bible for yourself, study to show yourself approved, and let the Spirit rightly divide the Word of Truth as you continue to seek elevation, growth, and development.

Jesus is very clear, direct, and bold throughout but for some reason people continue to get in their own way of the Truth.

The very issues that hindered the people's growth when Jesus was here are the same exact challenges that we are presented with today from the same groups of people.

A relationship with God does not consist of religion, rules, regulations, and the traditions of men nor does it promote condemnation, judgement, talebearing, backbiting, gossiping, jealousy, envy, or hate.

God is Love and God loves you.

How so very far we have separated ourselves from the Love of God due to our own ignorance, selfishness, greed, and failure to do due diligence and read the Bible for ourselves.

Discover the Gift of Truth that only God will provide and Simply Believe.

www.ingramcontent.com/pod-product-compliance
Lightning Source LLC
Chambersburg PA
CBHW072208070526
44585CB00015B/1243